My Route Adventure

© 2022 Michael Magee

All Rights Reserved

All rights reserved. No part of this publication may be reproduced, distributed, or transmitted in any form or by any means, including photocopying, recording, or other electronic or mechanical methods, without the prior written permission of the publisher, except in the case of brief quotations embodied in critical reviews and certain other noncommercial uses permitted by copyright law.

With thanks to

Kent Ford

Barbara and George at Gary's Gay Parita

Robert and Dawn Federico at The Blue Swallow Motel

Terry and Jerry of North Carolina

Martin and Mel fly drive explore

Stacey Andrews

And all those who have helped me along the way.

Dedicated to

Ros Magee, Jess Peacock, Ciaran, Lydia, & Reggie

The History of Route 66

U.S. Route 66 or **U.S. Highway 66** (**US 66** or **Route 66**) was one of the original highways in the United States Numbered Highway System. It was established on November 11, 1926, with road signs erected the following year. The highway, which became one of the most famous roads in the United States, originally ran from Chicago, Illinois, through Missouri, Kansas, Oklahoma, Texas, New Mexico, and Arizona before terminating in Santa Monica in Los Angeles County, California, covering a total of 2,448 miles (3,940 km).

It was recognized in popular culture by both the 1946 hit song "(Get Your Kicks on) Route 66" and the *Route 66* television series, which aired on CBS from 1960 to 1964. It was also featured in the Disney/Pixar animated feature film franchise *Cars*. In John Steinbeck's novel *The Grapes of Wrath* (1939), the highway symbolizes escape, loss, and the hope of a new beginning; Steinbeck dubbed it the **Mother Road**. Other designations and nicknames include the **Will Rogers Highway** and the **Main Street of America**.

US 66 was a primary route for those who migrated west, especially during the Dust Bowl of the 1930s, and it supported the economies of the communities through which it passed. People doing business along the route became prosperous, and they later fought to keep it alive in the face of the growing threat of being bypassed by the new Interstate Highway System.

US 66 underwent many improvements and realignments over its lifetime, but it was officially removed from the United States Highway System in 1985 after it was entirely replaced by segments of the Interstate Highway System. Portions of the road that passed through Illinois, Missouri, Oklahoma, New Mexico, and Arizona have been communally designated a National Scenic Byway by the name "**Historic Route 66**", returning the name to some maps. Several states have adopted significant bypassed sections of the former US 66 into their state road networks as State Route 66. The corridor is also being redeveloped into U.S. Bicycle Route 66, a part of the United States Bicycle Route System that was developed in the 2010s.

Now Route 66 would not of survived without one man Mr Angel Delgadillo, a Barber in Seligman Az.
After the decline and eventual delisting of the route from the United States Highway System in 1985, he went on to found the Historic Route 66 Association of Arizona. Eventually, route 66 associations were founded in all

eight US 66 states with a similar goal: preserving the once-important road.

While researching the history of Route 66 for the 2006 Pixar motion picture *Cars*, John Lasseter met Delgadillo, who told him how traffic through the town virtually disappeared on the day that nearby Interstate 40 opened. In the film, Sally Carrera (an animated gynomorphic Porsche 996 motorcar) serves as a vehicle to deliver that message in a 3½ minute flashback in which the town and the US Highway vanish literally from the map. It has been said that Delgadillo helped to inspire the movie through his passion for the road.

Over the years, he has become an attraction along the road with people stopping to talk to him and coming from all over the world just to meet him. When the Associated Press was interviewing him, he met with tourists from Europe and Asia.

For his work in promoting Route 66, Delgadillo has been called "The Father of the Mother Road," "The Guardian Angel of Route 66," and "The Ambassador." Angel's story has been immortalized in the song "Angel Delgadillo", written by former Kingston Trio member John Stewart on his album "Rough Sketches".

The Beginning

Picture this! Its 5.50pm and I'm watching the clock with tears in my eyes, sitting next to my partner Jess on the sofa, holding her hand while my children Ciaran and Lydia look blankly at me as this is one of the very few times I've allowed them to see me cry. At 6pm I will be picked up by my friend John whose going to take me to Bournemouth interchange to what will be the first leg of the biggest thing I've ever done in my life! Years in the planning, going over every little detail, looking at maps the history and working out what id like to see and put my time and money into over the things that I was not overly bothered to see.

This was my trip, my adventure and it was going to be done my way and not what some forum or book says I should.

But how did I get here right? I think its best we go back to the start and work our way from there. But don't worry you legend who's reading this it won't take long.

So back in the mid 80s on a Sunday afternoon I caught the beginning of a film being on this long road I found out was Route 66. I was hooked that there was a single road that went from Chicago to California. I actually thought it was one straight road, how wrong was I! Over the years growing up this road stuck in my mind, and I often spoke about it and how one day id be driving the route myself and completely alone.

As I grew older and started to get jobs with actually good money I never thought about doing the "trip of a lifetime" that visit to the mother road, I was too busy fucking around with multiple girlfriends, a CB radio, and a subscription to Max Power magazine. I followed a path into the world of the paranormal and for many fucking years this took more time and money than anything else.

After moving to Bournemouth I wanted to get myself sorted out and get my head down. With my 40th birthday a year away, it was time to get planning. I watched everything I could find on the route over and over, studying everything little detail. Being a coach driver for a few years I've become good with directions and studying maps. I was going to know the route and each town off by heart as a backup. Anyway I booked flights with British Airways did the Facebook posts and played the waiting game. The trip of a lifetime was booked; it was actually going to happen, and I was going on my own.

Ok back to the crying!

John was outside and it was time for me to go to the station. I was crying but not as hard as I wanted too, I was trying so hard not to but even with the trip I've wanted to do my whole life but my god I was going to miss Jess and the kids. Even looking down at Reggie the family dog the way he was just looking at me made me cry. I gave them all a kiss and big hugs and I was out the door with my Ray ban's on looking like a fat Bono as I dragged my case to Johns van. I was a total mess I got in the van and off we went to Bournemouth station to catch my service to Heathrow. Once I got to the station I started to feel much better, and even with the coach being an hour late I was doing ok. For years I've stopped my coach by the Hotel Sofitel, and seen the rich go inside this huge 5* hotel right inside Terminal 5 and as my treat I had booked a night inside the hotel so I'd be at the airport early and ready to go.

It was a long walk to the actual hotel and down a lift but when I got in it was stunning, I was being treated like I was someone, not this guy with more problems than a 90s ford fiesta.

As I booked in as I was there for my birthday I was given a free room upgrade and a free drink in the bar. I was so excited to see the room as I had not really stayed in a hotel many times before and being away from home was going to put me to the test. I found my room and was very happy with it. Worth the money? No id not say so but I was in the Terminal.

I went down to the restaurant and ordered the only thing on the menu that I knew I'd like a burger and chips. I sat there looking around and it was just pure money everywhere, I remember seeing a drunk American guy being flash with his money, and kept saying "it's only money". The food was really good and the ketchup came in little jars and was the best I've ever had!

A couple behind me were having a row and I sat there thinking I wonder if they will ever make up? After I paid for the food I made my way through to the bar for my free drink and I went with a pint of Corrs light. Now I'd never had this drink before as I'm more of an Irish whiskey drinker but it was really good. I sat alone in the corner in a bit of a daze wondering what was going to happen the next day. Now I can't begin to tell you how nervous I was walking back to my room, I was going to get to bed but I knew id not sleep. The TV was on in the background as I lay there desperate to get to sleep but my mind was racing.

Before I knew it the phone was ringing it was 6am. I jumped out of bed and into the shower thinking wow I'm actually doing this, I'm going on an adventure! I had a shower and got ready the whole time feeling on edge, missing my family and just the worry of the flight.

I made my way down to the reception checked out and made my way back down the long tunnels to terminal 5.

There was me thinking this was going to be easy, but British Airways made sure it was going to be a fucking pain in the dick.

At check in I was told I now had to download an app to help along the check in, and it happened to be the one part of the terminal I had no signal. After kicking up a fuss and being told "I don't care if you are 40 today we don't do free upgrades" they checked me in took my case and sent me on another 14,000 steps to the main security area. Here the only thing they didn't do was finger me. I had to take my belt off, my trainers off, they took everything out of my back pack as I stood there making sure my US dollars were still there, the fucking heat in the airport was a joke, I was sweating and not just because I'm a fat so, but it was actually hot.

I made it through security and I was now left to walk around the duty free, which I have to say is far from cheap. I actually found most things cheaper in local shops to me, gone are the times where you can save a few pound buying on holiday.

As I made my way to the gate I had to go down the longest escalators I've ever seen in my life! As I stood there going down and looking at how far they go I remember thinking "if someone fell down these they would be really fucked up".

I finally made it to the gate and I did the whole quick photo of the plane. We were called row by row of course the posh people first, going back to the people like me who have to watch every penny.

As I got on the plane I was met by the BA staff that were all big smiles and gave me a big welcome even though I was in the poor seats. They saw my I'm 40 badge (of course I had a plan B) and said "oh happy birthday" I carried on walking and said "oh thanks so much" and just carried on walking.

As I got to my seat I looked and thought oh fuck my life, it was the smallest area ever, even for a thin person.

As I got sat down and finally managed to get the belt on a flight steward came over and said "my boss would like to talk to you"

I thought BOOM premium seat time, but noooooooo!

I walked up and met the flight manager Sarah, who said to me

"as its your birthday and you have chosen us I have a gift for you" and gave me a smile.

"Follow me" she said now I will admit I was unsure at this point whether she meant a better seat or the mile high club? But the way I saw it, it was better than the poor seat. Sarah took me to BA Club world seats; she said "Here is a better seat to enjoy your birthday flight"

Now this was OUTSTANDING! The seat laid into a bed, I had my own area.

As I sat there looking at the free bag of goodies, pillow, and blanket not to mention the 4k TV with loads of films, a young lady said "would you like a glass of champagne?"

I looked up and it was the flight attendant who was going to be looking after me during the flight.

Her name was Ashley McQueen, a young Scottish lady and even though she knew I was part of the poor club she treated me like I was one of the club class gang.

Ashley gave me a glass of champagne and it was really that, a glass. Not like the plastic I was already mentally ready for.

As I sat there holding back the tears as things like this never EVER happen to me, Ashley came back collected my empty glass. Now I can't remember if it was before or after takeoff but Ashley gave me a menu with lunch options. I was in the Club gang, and even though Ashley knew I was out of my depth here she treated me like I was somebody. I don't think the staff of this BA flight will ever really know just how much it all meant to me!

Now if you have not flown in the BA club or above you need too!

I was drinking coke like I had never had it before, then the offer of tea, and getting a real nice mug of tea. I kept wanting to take my empty's up like I do when I'm out but the BA cabin crew were on the ball. I picked out my main meal, and to be honest it was an easy call for me as I have a saying "stick with what you know"

I went with a chicken pie, chocolate pudding and some red pepper stuff. I kept leaning up on my seat to look around to see everyone maybe in hope I could make a friend or see someone who is excited like me, but they all looked like pure money, this was not a new thing for them at all.

The food was out of this world, even the silverware and plate felt expensive. I just sat there eating in a daze a sort of shock that this was really happening to me, I was in a place I never thought I'd ever be able to afford or see myself, eating food id never normally choose but the flavours were just outstanding, and its made me less picky now as I've been missing out on so so much!

After all the food, drink, films and little nap in my chair bed we were landing!

Sarah the BA manager on board the flight gave me a birthday card and a bottle of champagne. At that point I just started crying as I'm not used to anyone outside of the family buying anything for me. These complete strangers made such an effort for my birthday flight and to make it just perfect!

I noticed people looking out of their windows and I heard a lady say "America below" now I never had a window seat so I got up to use the toilet and had a look outside via an empty seat. I looked out and could see land and according to the live feed on the TV screens we were not far away at all!

Again it hit me how much I was missing my family and I wanted them there with me, beside me to see it all with me, and I've never felt so selfish in my life!

But we had all had a long talk about me going and they were more than fine with me doing it alone and I was always talking about this big adventure along the mother road that I'd be doing on my own.

Looking back now I can't say id even considered what it would feel like doing such a trip on my own and I really should have thought about things.

The time had come we landed I was on American soil and the start of a trip that was going to change my life forever!

CHICHGO (Day 2)

I made it! I was in America land of the Karen's, the place I always wanted to see, experience the culture eat the fast food and take full advantage of everything I could.

I joined a HUGE line in O'Hare airport customs and I watched the flight crew from my flight walk to a separate area and I remember thinking right this is it, I'm well on my own now and the heat started to really kick in. Everywhere I looked someone had a badge and a gun and seemed to really be on the ball with the rules, I got shouted at for taking a photo.
I made my way through and even though I was on my own at this point I got through customs easy and fast. I got through the final stage and went to get my case, as I stood there a guy saw my birthday badge and shouted "HAPPY BIRTHDAY" across the hall and we got into conversation about my trip etc

I never got his name but I remember him telling me about his travels all over the world, he even looked like the typical free man, long hair, bracelets made of wood and string and I remember wanting to ask him if he was a vegan?

As he walked off I thought even some mates of mine never said happy birthday but a total stranger could take the time, and this was the very start of the wake up I needed. I started to see the world different I was locked into some sort of negative trap of only seeing the world through social media. But now I was away from my home in Dorset without the home comforts. Everyone around me was going someplace, and maybe an adventure of their own? I walked with my case through a little walk way then I was in the main entrance of the airport.
Now o2 told me they had sorted my phone so I could use it overseas but as I turned it on, NOTHING!
It was not working for outgoing calls so the first thing I did was used WhatsApp to call home and say I had landed ok and hearing their voices, the heat the I just don't know what I'm doing right now kicked in and I felt the stress and anxiety hit me. I looked around to see if anyone else were on their own but they all seemed to just be rushing around. I saw I was by the taxi bay, and got a taxi to the hotel.

Now I've been in a few shit cars in my time but this taxi was completely fucked. The guy put the hotel address in his phone and then we were off! He could hardly speak

English and was driving like the car was stolen; I opened the window to have this warm air hit me. The driver asked me to close it as he was cold to which I replied

"You're having a fucking laugh yeah?" he muttered something and we carried on. We were in traffic for most of the way, and I just looked out the window at the cars and vans, still in a little shock that I was really here and this was really happening. In hindsight I should of gone away for a few nights in the lead up to this trip, but I was here, and I was only going in one direction. I remember seeing a Pepsi lorry and getting a photo of it as it was the first time I'd seen one for real and not in the background of a Hollywood movie, I almost said to the driver "look a Pepsi lorry" but this was just the norm for him, I had no one to tell and point it out, something I'd have to get used to while I was here.

$70 later we made it to the waldorf astoria Chicago, I was met by a member of hotel staff who opened my door while another was getting my bags out the boot of the Taxi. I made my way into the reception the whole time my heart beating out my chest, I looked around at the fixtures and fittings of this 5* hotel that would be my home for the night. It was absolutely immaculate as was the staff in their uniforms, this was my treat to myself.

I was met by a guy maybe late 20's and looked like he should be in love island. A tall man with a chiselled jaw and hair straight from Nicky Clark himself.

"welcome to the Waldorf Astoria Chicago Mr Magee, I believe its you're 40th birthday"

"Yes it is" I said I was just about to ask how he knew then I remembered I was wearing a 40th birthday badge, and that little badge did it again....

"were upgrading you Mr Magee to a much bigger suit"

BOOM ! Another upgrade I was going to make the most out of this!

They asked for a credit card to take a $250 deposit, now I can't say I'm used to hotels but EVERY HOTEL and MOTEL in the USA charge. I gave my card and it was rejected. So I tried again and again it was declined.

By chance a month before I flew out my bank offered me a 2nd credit card with no overseas fees, and it was this card that worked.

I made my way to the 19th floor and opened the door to what was the best hotel room id ever been in. I put my bags down and tried to call home and found my car was not working, but more on this later. I got myself on the hotel wifi and used messenger to video call home. The second Jess picked up I broke down crying, I was missing the family way more than I could ever of imagined. After talking for around 45 minutes we hung up and I decided to take a walk around Chicago and get a drink or something I could keep in my room. I went down and I made my way to the Bean (Cloud Gate) now the heat was unreal, I was still in my jeans and shirt and thought I'd be ok but the heat was really getting to me.

I went into a small local shop and brought a drink and carried on my way. I came across a 7-11 and thought id pop in and check it out, now this must be the most ghetto shop I've ever been inside, I brought some chocolate a bottle of Pepsi and a big bottle of water and it came to $14.00 to say I was shocked was an understatement but I never said anything I paid and carried on. Now I think we have all heard the stories of never drink hot drinks on a plane, but it never hit me till the worst possible thing happened. As I was maybe 200 meters from the bean everything I had eaten and drank in the last 24 hours wanted to burst out my arse!

This could not have happened at a worse place, I just didn't know what to do, so I carried on walking towards the bean in hope of this feeling passing till I was at the hotel.

I had to ask for directions a few times but I managed to find it. Now this was not what I was expecting at all! The Bean was amazing to see but smaller than I thought it would be, the area around it however was filled with unsavoury looking people and a small group of drug users that were making a lot of noise. I was not expecting this at all as all the videos I had seen on it, it looked like a posh area. Out the corner of my eye I saw the gift shop and toilets. I made a point of walking towards it as fast as I could, the whole time thinking how much better id feel, and still reminding myself that I was in the USA about to start Route 66.

I swung the gents door open like I owned the place and walked in to find that this toilet was filled with people and I don't mean going to the toilet but what looked like a drug user and a few homeless people washing, now I was in that bad a state I just walked past them to find the toilet doors were nothing like the UK.

In fact they were that small if I sat down I could of had a chat with the homeless guy washing his socks. At this point it had got quiet and I was the centre of attention, and I'm sure if it wasn't for my size id put money on it id of been robbed. I got out of there and made my way back to the hotel as quick as I could, trying my best to look at the buildings and the shops but also trying my hardest not to shit myself.

I was able to get Google maps working on my phone and it helped me get back to the hotel.

After taking the best shit in the world I again found myself looking in the mirror with such a huge amount of emotions and thoughts running through my head. I looked at myself; this hot sweaty guy all red faced and just said "what were you thinking"

I sat down on the bed and had the balcony door open for the fresh air, and started to flick through the TV channels seeing celebs doing adverts for credit cards and food companies. I had a few glasses of pepsi and got a shower, looking back now I wish I got in the HUGE bath I had but my mind was all over the place. After I came out closed the curtains and just went to sleep, this was around 6pm but I was so overwhelmed I just wanted to sleep it off. I woke up at 4am and sat outside on the balcony, then I heard "pop pop pop" I didn't think anything of it till I heard the police pulling up and blocking off a road close to the hotel. I then checked my phone as I was due a refund onto one of my credit cards, the one that was declined at the hotel reception and I saw it had been refunded BUT my accounts had been blocked.

Again the panic kicked in and as soon as I left the hotel I did not have access to the internet as it was so on and off.

Thank to every god ever that Natwest bank has an app, and on the app you can video chat.

I went on the app and managed to talk to a lady called Claire Withers. NOW she was AMAZING!! She could see that the credit card side of Natwest had blocked it for security as the small 70 cents check on the card triggered the security team. Even though I had told the bank 6 months before id be in the USA they still blocked it. Claire contacted the credit card team on my behalf and told them to contact me, which they did and everything was finally sorted. But without the help of Claire Withers id of been in major trouble! But more of that much later on.

I was due to get my car at 9am and I was watching the time just wanting to get started I sat on the bed watching American TV and eating American chocolate, knocking back more and more Pepsi. In the back of my mind I knew this would be the most liberating thing I'll ever do and I'm about to go on an adventure, but I was missing my family real bad at this point and I felt so selfish for doing this on my own.

As I was getting my bags ready I noticed I had gotten chocolate on the bed sheets so I left a note and in hindsight I should of worded it different but I left a very simple "chocolate not shit" note followed by a "sorry"

I went to the reception where the staffs were fussing around me like vultures wanting their tips. They called me a taxi to take me to the Hertz car hire. It was much cooler and I was in the right let's do this shit mode. As I walked into this small building I was just hoping it would all be ok, id have some amazing car but there was an error. Now let's back track a bit so you understand. I did have a car booked with SIXT but a week before I flew out I had a bad feeling that I needed more money and in a blind panic I cancelled this car and got refund of $2100 I then booked with Hertz and got a car for $1100 so I was now a grand better off. However with the time delays and the booking systems in the UK talking to the USA I never had the car I thought I was getting. I was given the option of waiting in the office till a car came back, was checked and cleaned and could be a whole day wait or take the only car they had left

A 1.0 litre Chevrolet spark. I took it! And it was the best choice I could have ever made. Now she was small so much so I had trouble getting my suitcase into the boot, I put my 24 stone body into this car and it even moved an inch, she was strong and after many years of company cars and professional driving I had a good feeling about this car. I took the car out of the garage and pulled up in this dark dingy alleyway and got out to look around her. I said out loud "were doing Route 66" I got back into the car and made my way to a petrol station as it was almost empty. The chevy was so easy to drive, I was expecting some sort of crap driving on the left side but it's so much better than the UK. I found a gas station and decided to use my card on this one as I just wanted to get started. I filled her up and all she took was $49.55 around £42.64. I was VERY happy with this!

From there I wanted to go have breakfast is the world famous Lou Mitchell's. Lou Mitchell's, also known as Lou Mitchell's Restaurant, is a Chicago diner located at 565 W. Jackson Boulevard. It is a popular restaurant for commuters, as it is located near Union Station. It is also located near the start of U.S. Route 66 and was frequented by many people at the start of their journey along the road, earning it the nickname "the first stop on the Mother Road." In May 2002, the Nationwide Route 66 restoration program was launched at Lou Mitchell's. It was listed on the National Register of Historic Places in 2006. This was going to be my first stop for breakfast, and to see the start point for many doing the route so I thought id pop in. I found a car park and made my way there. I had a Greek sausage special with fried potatoes, and it came with a little doe ball which tasted AMAZING. From there I made my way through the streets of Chicago to the Willis tower to visit the sky deck. It opened in 1973 as the world's tallest building, a title that it held for nearly 25 years. It is currently the third-tallest building in the Western Hemisphere, as well as the 23rd-tallest in the world. Each year, more than 1.7 million people visit the Skydeck observation deck, the highest in the United

States, making it one of Chicago's most popular tourist destinations. I'd seen Billy Connelly stop by in his Route 66 show and I really wanted to see it for myself.

It was a bit of a walk and a pain to find but the staff on site were really helpful. At the start of the tour you get to walk around a sort of expedition of Chicago with the history and so much information. So that and on top the sky deck only cost me $36.00. After the walk through I got in the lift to the 99th floor then another to the 103rd floor, my ears were popping on the way up.

There's a glass box 1.5 inches thick stopping me falling to my death, it was so good to just stand there and look down to the pavement outside that I had just walked along, the view was out of this world it really was breath taking seeing the whole of Chicago while walking around the sky deck. They took a photo of me up there and as a treat to myself I brought it, I think it was $20 or so I can't really remember but as I was on my adventure I thought why not, I normally avoid these things back in the UK, maybe it was the altitude or jetlag but I'm glad I got it. I went to the gift shop back in the basement and brought a magnet and made my way back to the car. After a short time I was back at the car park and I put my ticket into the paying machine and saw what felt like a slap round my face the cost!

They wanted $53.00 around £46.00 at the time for just over an hour and 30 minutes. I was really pissed off at the costs but thought ok just pay and let's make my way to the next stop the Official Route 66 start sign. I pulled up and just stood there looking at it, this was it I was here I was actually doing it. I took some photos and video for my YouTube channel and I was away and heading towards the next stop of my trip and one I was looking forward too, The Launching pad home of The Gemini Giant. Now this took around an hour and just as I got out of the city it started to rain and rain real hard.

As I got close I could see the giant from a distance and it felt great to finally see it in person, and I was so glad I was out of Chicago.

I popped inside and brought myself a large Coke and sat down taking it all in; from the seats to the rock n roll music playing. An old lady sat there looking at me while I filmed around maybe wondering what I was doing?

I got my Route 66 passport stamped by a young kid, and before I knew it I was back on the road and headed towards Pontiac and see the museum and Bob waldmire's old bus.

The museum was just amazing, it had an older lady with white hair greet me and made me feel very welcome, I took my time walking around looking at everything and got to see Bob's bus which was the inspiration for Flo in Disney cars.

I met a few people from the north of the UK, who were also keeping out of the rain and I spent a while talking to them and we all agreed that it was a lot more expensive than we thought it would be, and talked about when and how long for we should use the I40. The I40 is a major road that runs from the east coast to the west almost. I made a point of staying on the mother road as much as I could but if I was running behind, low on petrol, of felt like it was getting too late to be out on the unlit roads then I'd be on the I40.

Outside the rain was so hard and cold I was able to see another of Bob Waldmire's home an old school bus he had converted and lived in and would drive Route 66 up and down often.

Now here I should let you know who Bob Waldmire is for those who don't know, In fact I'm still learning things about him.

Bob Waldmire (April 19, 1945–December 16, 2009) was an American artist who is well known for his artwork of U.S. Route 66. Being the son of Ed Waldmire Jr., he is often associated with the Cozy Dog Drive In restaurant in Springfield, Illinois (on U.S. Route 66), where the elder Waldmire (along with his friend Don Strand) created the corn dog.

Waldmire was a well-known snowbird, spending his winter months in Arizona's Chiricahua Mountains in a self-sufficient home of his own design. During the summer, he travelled the country, but based himself in his native Central Illinois, living in a converted Chevrolet school bus near Springfield.

In 2004, Bob Waldmire was given the John Steinbeck Award because of his contributions to the preservation of Route 66.

On December 16, 2009, Waldmire died from cancer.

Bob was like the god father of Route 66 everyone knew him and no matter where you go on the route he's still spoken of, well loved and very much missed.

Anyway back to the adventure..

The rain was even more heavy and it took out my phone signal so I was completely lost but I saw a sign saying west so I took it and by chance I saw a sign Old Route 66, so I carried on and after a few miles I saw the I40 running alongside me, I saw a sign to say I was entering Lexington, I was worried about getting lost and decided to buy a sat nav at a Wal-Mart when I found one. I carried along Route 66 looking out for treasures along the route that I could maybe stop at and before I knew it

I was at a town called Normal and a little old gas station called "Ryburn Place" Now the Route 66 passport said this was open on the day but it turns out it was closed and the times and days in the passport were wrong.

I did meet an English couple called Andy and Alene who were in a top speck Ford Mustang and were coming from the West to finish in Chicago. It was so good meeting them we had a great chat about things and they said it was a bit cheaper in the west and had all the same worries as I did, which made me feel sooooo much better.

A couple of American bikers pulled up and I had a little chat with them which was nice.

It was then time for me to jump back on the mother road and I carried on along Route 66. I was thinking about how nice it was too of seen a few Brits on my way.

As I was driving I started to feel unwell, a little sick and in need of a toilet. Now I don't deal with sickness well at the best of times but being in a different country on my own just made me feel even worse. As I was picking up speed along Route 66 I saw a sign for one of my stops, Funks Grove. This could not have come at a better time as I was already thinking about just pulling over.

I pulled into funks grove and as I parked up I looked to my right and saw a porter toilet, now this was a gift from the gods and I just ran over and went, I felt so much better I walked into the gift shop like I was high on drugs trying all the maple syrup and local honeys.

After picking up a few gifts to take home I was back on the mother road heading towards my next stop the Bunyon man in Atlanta, and the timing could not of been better. As I stood there looking a gentleman came behind me and said "would you like me to take a photo for you" At first I said no as I felt a little sad being on my own and didn't want to really start a chat, but I then said "actually would you mind?" and he did. His brother came up and they introduced themselves and Terry and Jerry, twins from North Carolina who were doing the route for their 60th birthday. They were so nice and said they had spent a night or 2 in their Tesla due to how expensive the hotels were.

After a little while I was back on my way again filled with happiness that I had spoken to more people on the route.

The radio was loud and after a drive I was at the hotel for the night, and I was so glad I made it!

I checked into the Country inn and suites hotel in Springfield Illinois.

I checked in and went to my room, and it was really nice, not much of a view just the gas station next door. I went out and found a McDonalds and got a take away, and on my way back stopped off in the gas station for drinks and anything that looked good. I walked around with no idea of what to eat so ended up with a 3 musketeer bar which is now my fave American chockolet bar and went back to my room. I was woken around 4am with the worst pain in my belly but after a toilet run I was able to get back off to sleep till 7am.

Now im not that sure what it was but if you're in the area id give the McDonalds a miss.

Illinois (Day 2)

My alarm went off and I made my video calls back home the whole time trying not to cry as I missed them so much. I had a shower and took all the free bits from the bathroom. I had already done this back in Chicago and my plan was to do this the whole route and when I got back send them to my mate Liam Matthew as he would have thought it was a great gift, and a private joke from a trip we took to Birmingham.

My plan for the day to start was the Cozy Dog drive in for breakfast then head over to the actual home of Abraham Lincoln for a tour and I was so excited about it, I had seen a video of this place many years earlier and I just really wanted to walk around on the wooden sidewalks looking at the old houses that had not been changed since Mr. Lincoln himself lived there.

As I got outside the hotel I noticed a huge power station in the distance and it made me giggle that this could be the Springfield the Simpsons were based on. I drove to the Cozy dog to try my first ever corn dog I was looking around at all the different shops, and the big yellow school busses. A school bus was in front of me as I drove, and I'll always remember this little girl maybe 7 or 8 dancing away at the back of the bus in a flower style dress, she looked so happy on her way to school and I remember thinking I hope that feeling never goes away for her.

The Cozy dog was really nice; it was filled with information on Route 66, and a little gift shop. I brought a Cozy dog and a Coke and sat down and took in the history of the building. I never stayed here too long as I was the only one eating and I had so much to do, so I headed to the Lincoln home historic site. Abraham Lincoln was the 16th president of the USA and his house is still standing and you can go look around inside. As I pulled up to the car park it was already getting busy, I got out and the heat just hit me, it was just a case of getting used to the heat in America, but by the time I got to the main building it was ok and never seemed to bother me as much as it did getting out of the car. I brought a ticket for the 9.30 tour and sat down and waited. It was such a strange feeling being there, I kept thinking of all the years I wanted to see the USA and now I was here, it was so exciting. The staff at the Lincoln historic site are just OUTSTANDING. They all said hello when passing and took interest in me being from the UK and I was made to feel very welcome. We met our guide and he gave a talk giving the history of the Lincoln home, and area, and I have to admit it was very interesting. Now something strange happened to me that's never happened before and I hope never happens again. As we stood around listing to the guide I was stood under a tree as I prefer the shade but for some reason I wanted a better view of the house and moved into the sun. A matter of seconds after I moved a branch large enough to of put me in the hospital fell from the tree and landed right where I was stood. It went completely silent and the guide looked at me and said "well you don't see that every day" I just stood there looking between the branch and him and all I could think of was the film Final Destination. We soon made our way up to the Lincoln house and it is just stunning, and when you stand there looking at its beauty you need to remember that this house is from 1844 and is still in brand new condition. The walkways all around the home and streets are all made of wood which I thought were great, as it was so much more authentic for the time. We were then taken inside the home and given a tour of it, and I could not believe just how nice it was, a lot had of course changed but the home still boosted Abraham Lincoln's original desk and chair among other items and the kitchen was untouched. As we were about to leave the kitchen area out of the corner of my eye I thought I had seen someone walk past a door which gave me chills and when I asked the guide if this was a thing that's happened before he refused to talk about it. More than likely just a trick of the light but I do hope I had seen something in the house. From there I walked around the homes that are part of the tour for an hour and took the time to call home then I called my lifelong friend Stacey Andrews who was on holiday in morocco, crazy how far technology has come. I then made my way into St Louis to see the arch. The drive was real long and I had the air con on full, as I saw the St Louis arch I made it into the second county Missouri. Now for anyone who's not been before St Louis is not the safest of places, and I was still hours away from my next hotel so I decided to stop at Ted Drewes for some frozen custard which is a very popular stop for everyone on the route.

I was not sure how it worked but a local lady explained to me how you order and what is best but I chose a chocolate and caramel and it tasted so good! It had a huge line of people waiting for their frozen treat but I can say it's worth it even in the heat.

It's been trading since 1929 and I can see why, it was cheap, great size cups and so much to choose from, I really wanted to share this with the family and again missed them so much!

I headed again on the mother road towards my stop for the night Cuba Missouri which is just outside St Louis, as it was way cheaper and safer.

I found the super 8 hotel and checked in, and I had a view of the car park so I could see my hire car and I had a ice machine outside my room. I called home via video call and again felt sad, but this area was the real start of what I like to call "nice America" I found the locals in the east not to be very nice at all but the further west you go the nicer they are.

This was the biggest problem that at night in the USA I was alone as everyone back home was asleep and I found that hard, but started to enjoy American TV. Now it was that time that I needed food and I was craving fruit, so I headed out in the car to see what was around and after a short time I found a supermarket. Now this was not on any tourist route and was just filled with locals, it was a fun sight to see, I walked around and for the first time I could really feel American life. I found the fruit and veg section and it looked so good, so much to choose from and all kept inside a chillier. I grabbed some apples and bits for the kids to take home and made my way to the till. The young guy who served me had a real thick American accent and seemed a little taken back when I started talking to him. We spoke about my trip and what I was hoping to get from it, he wished me luck and I was on my way. On my way back I found a Walmart. This was the first time I had been in one and after hearing all about it from my daughter who has seen it on YouTube I was actually excited to go in and check it out. They sold clothing that fit me and it was cheap! I stocked up on t-shirts and boxers and even found a large tub of Flintstone gummies. I again got talking to some of the staff who said it was nice to see a tourist as it was rare they had anyone from the UK go in. This visit turned out to be a blessing, as most of my American dollars were in $100 bills, and I saw they had a self service check out so took the opportunity to use one of them to get smaller bills. I later found out it was not a big deal at all having a large cash note like in the UK. After I went to the Pizza Hut next door to the hotel and I thought was closed at first but it turned out it was take away only. I went in and ordered a medium ham and pepperoni and had a chat with the staff as they were not used to seeing as English guy at all and was surprised that I was not staying in St Louis. I got my pizza and went to my room and it actually tasted much better than the UK, and it was a little tick off the list. As a kid I wanted an American Pizza hut after seeing it so often in films. After eating I just lay there on the bed watching TV flicking through all the channels thinking of my family at home sleeping. I had an early night and slept so well, it was one of the best hotels on the route that I stayed in.

Missouri (Day 3)

I woke up at 6.30am and called home feeling a lot better about things, and as always on this trip day times were amazing, the nights more lonely.

I looked out the window to see that it had been raining over night and I was glad of the cooler weather. As I looked down at my hire car I was now calling Chevy chev, I thought to myself how the hell am I doing this is a car that must be the smallest on any American road, I was starting to like this car!

I packed all my things and checked out, and in true style having to go back to the room to collect the apples that I had got the night before. My first stop was a lot closer than I thought it would be the Fanning outpost.

Now this one I was really looking forward too as Billy Connolly had stopped off and I was really looking forward to see the world's largest rocking chair, that doesn't actually rock.

As I pulled up it was very quiet and with a cool breeze, I stood and looked up at the non rocking chair thinking of Billy himself sitting up on it laughing away. I went inside the general store and it was filled with every sort of fizzy drink, pop corn and Route 66 gift you could think of, this place was huge.

Now at this point I was still getting used to filming myself but as it was so quiet I was well away filming myself like I knew what I was doing. I brought a few magnets and got the passport stamped and made my way back to the car.

As I carried on up the mother road I came across a vulture eating some road kill, I was shocked to see this as I had only seen them in cartoons and the odd film. I slowed the car down to look but they flew away, then as I looked up I saw Tortuous.

I parked up to look at them they were just baby ones I did what I could to pick them up and move them off the road, I'd never seen a real one in the wild before let alone picking them up.

I carried on and made my way to the Devil's elbow bridge.

It was quiet just with the sounds of insects, not a person in site, it was just so majestic standing here looking at the river flowing under the bridge, thinking about how many people had been here seeing this for the first time either making their way west for a better start or those like me on Route 66 to get our kicks.

It was time for me to move on to my next stop "Uranus".

Now Uranus is a mix of fun strange things, a freak show attraction, fudge factory and home to the world's biggest belt buckle.

As soon as I got out the car I was face to face with an old London bus parked up with a plastic skeleton in the driver's seat. This was a welcome site and I hoped to see some English people here as the car park was packed. I walked road the side to see a stage and just really random things like models of aliens and fun posters.

They had 3 mannequins of a hillbilly band on a stage I thought were funny. As I walked up I saw a gift shop that had a "side show" in the back. As I walked in I was met by a large lady with what looked like head to toe tattoos that made her look more like an animal. She asked me if I wanted to see the side show for $5.00. "course I do why not, where is it?" I said to her. She gave a small smile and said "five bucks". I gave her the money and she pointed to a door in the back. Now at this point I did wonder if I had just fucked myself and I was about to walk through a door into a Mandingo party where I was going to be the piggy. I pushed it open to see a huge room and directly in front of me was a Fiji mermaid, and the head of a dog man. I thought ok as long as they don't need a fat man display I think I'll be ok. I walked around and it was very clean and neat and everything in its place. As I got to the middle of the room a family came in which made me feel better. They had a 2 headed turtle in a tank and it was so strange to see but I suppose this is what this exhibition was all about.

The tattooed lady came in and offered to swallow a sword for me. Now at this point I was not actually sure what she meant and if she really meant a sword or something sexual. The she held out a sword so that cleared that one up for me, and as she was getting ready and asking the other family to come over I remembered the series American horror story "freak show" and got the giggles as they were all really trying hard and if they were actors they were really good!

The tattooed lady got set up in the corner and oiled up her sword and was ready!

We gathered round the outstanding air con they had going and got ready to see a true side show, show and I have to say I was excited as I'd never been to a side show before and it was such a great deal for what I was getting.

She gave details on the history of sword swallowing from around the world with a few jokes in between that no one really understood but we did a laugh anyway. The she did it, she picked up the sword and all the way down her throat it went, but she did not stop there! Noooo she leaned forward and gave herself an electric shock, a big blue bolt of electric was hitting the sword, then she took it out and that was it, I'd just seen something I'd never seen before, and until I see the mother road again I don't think I want too.

I came out in a sort of shock as what I had just seen and felt kind of awkward at the same time, but in true me style I saw a big gift shop so made the choice to put Kat the sword lady behind me and go see what I could see.

I walked into a small lobby area then through a second door to the gift shop where again I was hit with the most amazing air con and the second I actually got inside all the staff at the same time shouted "WELCOME TO URANUS" which was a total shock for me but I laughed and carried on looking around. I found some funny t-shirts which I brought and I took my time walking around trying to find things to take my mind off being sad about doing this on my own, the whole shop was filled with happy families with the odd loud "I SAID NO" and "PUT THAT BACK YOU ALREADY GOT SWEETS"

I paid for the gifts I brought and made my way outside but thought while I'm here, I went round and walked into the gift shop again so I could hear them shout "WELCOME TO URANUS" one last time.

As I walked to the car it started to get real hot now and I only had one more stop on my route today on the mother road, but a very long drive to and from the next attraction.

I got in the car and made a quick call home as I was really missing jess and the kids and I tried to act like normal but inside my heart was breaking, I felt so alive doing an American road trip on my own so liberated but so heartbroken my family were not with me.

I felt better getting off the phone and I headed to the next stop, Gary's Gay Parita.

Gary's Gay Parita is a vintage Sinclair gas station that was Founded in 1934, and is still open thanks to the efforts of the late Gary Turner, and has since been taken over by Gary's daughter Barb and her husband George. Now this place looks like true American pie with its neon signs and classic look, and is one of the Route 66 icons on the route. Now I had heard about this place many years ago and had seen photos of the gas station and the most beautiful restored yellow truck in a side barn or garage. I pulled up driving over a huge Route 66 sign painted in the road the whole time in shock that I was here, I was seeing the gas station in person and not in a video or photo. I pulled up past some traffic cones that had been placed around as filming was going on inside about a perfect looking lorry that was still in full time use, I thought it was on loan from a museum.

I was standing outside the gate waiting for them to finish filming before I went in and I felt like a kid just waiting to get in.

I got the nod and off I went inside to look around and I went over to Barb who was in the little gift shop at this point and said hello, I brought a few things then I was invited to sit with Barb and George and a few other locals and they treated me like I was a family member, they were asking me questions about where I was from my family etc and I felt at ease for the first time since getting to America, not like I would be at home but I was sitting outside on a bench on a porch with real Americans talking away like I had known them for years, and I really needed that. George said "let me give you a tour". Now this made me feel great and he took me to the original office of Gary Turner and showed me around, it was filled with photos and the history was bursting out the walls with its complete UN touched history, this was breathtaking and George told me the history and information about the gas station over the years. I mentioned that I had seen a yellow vintage truck that was restored to mint condition on the internet and he looked at me with a smile and said "follow me I'll show you" George and I took our time walking over to the side garage or barn I'm not sure what the building would be called, but on the way he was telling me what was what showed me the home he lives with Barb and the times on the perfectly cut lawn. I turned round and there it was, and it was beautiful. George stood in the door way and told me to take my time and look around. It was filled with Americana and classic signage and if I was not in a huge rush for my next stop id of stayed here much longer. Now this place was free to enter I was shocked at the fact that they just wanted to let people like me doing route 66 in and give a tour and tell you the history without an entry fee. Before I left George said "go help yourself to water, ice cream and I think there's still watermelon" this too was free for those who were coming to see this OUTSTANDING place. What I never knew at this point was George was just about to really save me later on, but we will get to that. They had a tip box on the wall by the gift shop so I put a nice donation in and if I could of id of donated 5 times as much as not only did I get tour of the gas station and classic cars all over the site and got to see in person the vintage Ford truck I got to sit down with local Americans and chat away on a porch like in the movies, and I really needed that. I got 2 bottles of water out a big fridge and got back on the road. One thing I did notice was the shops on Route 66 seem to close early, so if you take the mother road keep this in mind. I started to feel really hot and very sick and pulled into a town called Carthage not feeling well at all. I got out the car and went to a shop sort of shaking but it was closed. Now at this point I was in a bit of a panic then I remembered the water George and Barb gave me so I went back to the car and drank both bottles of cold water back to back and I instantly felt so much better! If George never said go get some bits I really don't know what had happened to me. I set off to Tulsa to find my hotel and get some food.

I got lost even with a sat nav on my phone working and found myself on some back road and I put my foot down a little stupidly and before I knew it I had run a stop sign with a truck on the other side looking completely shocked but I was going too fast to stop, and it shook me up enough that I didn't speed for the rest of the trip.

I finally got to the hotel and it was bad outside, directly opposite was a rough looking group of people hanging around but they didn't take much notice of me at all so I went inside got my room sorted and just sat there not really hungry but I had been driving for 5 hours in total so opted for a subway. I sat in my room looking at the time thinking that all my family and friends were fast asleep but I put the TV on and watched Blades of glory, and I have to say it was a comfort. The hotel was very loud with the sounds of a guy wanting a refund for a service he paid for, the sounds of a fight in the car park outside my window, and the whole time I lay in bed wondering if Chevy chev was ok?

Oklahoma (Day 4)

The morning could not have come fast enough! And today was a day I was REALLY looking forward to, I was going to see one of the most iconic attractions on the route.
The **Blue Whale of Catoosa** is a waterfront structure, just east of the American town of Catoosa, Oklahoma, and it has become one of the most recognizable attractions on old Route 66.

Hugh Davis built the Blue Whale in the early 1970s as a surprise anniversary gift to his wife Zelta, who collected whale figurines. The Blue Whale and its pond became a favoured swimming hole for both locals and travellers along Route 66 alike.
Originally, the pond surrounding the massive Blue Whale was spring fed and intended only for family use. However, as many locals began to come to enjoy its waters, Davis brought in tons of sand, built picnic tables, hired life guards, and opened it to the public. This was a short drive from the hotel and I was really excited to see it but before I see this icon of the mother road It was time for breakfast.
I pulled up at a Wendy's drive through and got their version of a mc muffin. I was asked if I wanted a large meal and needing a new cup for my Pepsi on the route I

chose this option. When I got the meal I was handed a HUGE 40oz cup with ice cold coke, a sausage and egg with cheese inside what they call a biscuit and a HUGE packet of fried potato bits. I pulled up enjoying how cool it was even though it was 7.30am I was wondering how hot it was going to get that day. I struggled to eat the meal and the drink lasted me hours. I made my way over to the Blue whale and when I got there it was around 8am and you could hear a pin drop! I walked closer just staring at the thing I'd seen on the internet and TV for many many years!

It was such a surreal experience being here, it reminded me of the 90s America you would see on the TV, I walked around on the inside filming and looking around so happy to be here. There was a steel ladder inside that took you to a second level, and I popped up to have a look hoping there were no homeless living in it.

I walked around the whole area taking a few photos from different angles just taking it all in, hoping that one day id be able to return to see it again but more of a just in case I never get to come back I just wanted to really experience it. It really is one of the one off attractions that you come across in life and never see anything like it again. From here I went to see the golden driller,

The **Golden Driller** is a 75-foot-tall (23 m), 43,500-pound (19,700 kg) statue of an oil worker, in Tulsa, Oklahoma. The structure is a steel frame covered with concrete and plaster. It is the sixth-tallest statue in the

United States and has been located in front of the Tulsa Expo Centre since 1966.

Now as I was driving round Tulsa I noticed just how beautiful the buildings are here, the detail was unreal. The heat started to build up as I pulled up at the Golden driller, I got out had a look and took a few photos and I was back on the road, I wanted to see the golden driller but it's not something you need to spend more than 5 minutes at.

From here I was going to another location Pop's Soda ranch.

Pops restaurant in Arcadia, Oklahoma is a modern roadside attraction on Route 66. Using a theme of soda pop, it is marked by a giant neon sign in the shape of a soda pop bottle. The glass walls of the restaurant are decorated with shelves of soda pop bottles, arranged by beverage colour. These bottles are for sale as-is, or may be purchased cold from the huge refrigerator at the western end.

Opened in 2007, the restaurant's structure incorporates a cantilevered truss extending 100 feet over the gas pumps and parking area in the forecourt.

The roadside sign is 66 feet tall and weighs 4 tons. The height is a reference to the historic highway beside which it is situated. Although apparently constructed from neon tubes, it is actually lit by LEDs, which provide a spectacular light show each night.

The establishment was owned by the late Oklahoman oil and gas magnate Aubrey McClendon and was designed by the noted architecture firm Elliott + Associates Architects. Pops has won several architectural awards. As I approached pop's I noticed to my right the Round barn. This is a place that's popped up many times but it's not something that I've had on a list of to do while I was on the route.

Now for some reason I pulled over at the last second and went inside to have a look. It was free to go inside and look around and it gave the history but also seemed to be selling old clothing like a jumble sale, I was only inside for a 10 minuets but that was enough for me. I jumped in the car and made the very short drive up the road to pops. The heat was almost too much for me so I got inside as quick as I could to be back in the comfort zone of air conditioning.

This place was great everywhere I looked there were every flavour of fizzy drinks you could think of, on top names I'd never even heard of even crazy ones.

I sat down for lunch and shocked myself by ordering a chicken salad and fries. They brought my food with a pot of their homemade BBQ sauce. I put the sauce to the side and made a start and it was so good not only that this was the first time in my 40 years I had ordered a salad, but the feeling of eating real food. It seemed hard to find a more healthy meal on the route as it was all burgers, stakes etc.

I put the pops homemade BBQ sauce on the food and it was possibly the best I've ever had! They should be selling this in bottles, I asked my waiter for another and he brought me one over, I had that with the fries it was so tasty! After paying my bill I went into the Pop's gift shop to look at all the bottles of pop. I got a box that held 6 bottles and did a deal they had on any 6 bottles.
After paying I went to the car and I noticed off in the distance Terry and Jerry who I had made friends with back in Pontiac.
I went over to see them and was given such a welcome, they had just made friends with 3 locals April, Linda and Deb. It was so good us all chatting away I needed that human connection I had been on my own for the longest time in my life and just that little chat and laugh made me feel alive. I look at Terry and Jerry as friends for life now.
Driving for hours on end was something I'm used to being a coach driver but it was starting to kick in now and I was getting tired of driving. I had one more stop on the route the Sandhill Curiosity Shop that's not actually a shop and it's not even on route 66 it's on a road that runs off of it. The little town in Erick looked like it had been left behind in the 90s; it was run down and looked like it had given up.
Harley the owner of the Sandhills shop that doesn't sell anything was known to be a "real hill Billy" in the sense of his crude ways of talking and only entertaining white

people. I pulled up looking round thinking what a dive this place is, I saw Harley and I went over and said hello. He was very rude to me and for the purpose of the book I won't put in his words but I was shocked!
I walked back to the car really pissed off that for the last 2 years I've been seeing him in videos playing music and having a laugh with those on the mother road and I get there to be spoken to like total shit!
Not wanting this to put a negative dent in the trip I brushed it off and carried on west, but this time I was going to skip the next few miles of route 66 and head on the I40 to the "Welcome To Texas" sign.
I was able to pull over by the sign to take photos and a German guy who had also stopped agreed to take my photo at the sign if I did his after. The heat was unreal here and I was glad to get back into Chevy Chev with its ice cold air conditioning. I carried on for what felt like forever but I finally made it to the town of Shamrock the home of the U drop inn. After getting set up in my hotel I took a walk around the corner to see the neon lights of the 1936 U drop inn.
The **U-Drop Inn,** also known as **Tower Station and U-Drop Inn** and **Tower Café,** was built in 1936
in Shamrock, Texas along the historic Route 66 highway in Wheeler County. Inspired by the image of a nail stuck in soil, the building was designed by J. C. Berry. An unusual example of art deco architecture applied to a gas station and restaurant, the building features two flared

towers with geometric detailing, curvilinear massing, glazed ceramic tile walls, and neon light accents. It has traditionally held two separate business: "Tower Station," a gas station on the western side, and the "U-Drop Inn," a café on the eastern side. Though it has passed hands several times in its history, the building has consistently housed the same types of businesses it was originally constructed for.

Once considered a beautiful and impressive example of Route 66 architecture in Texas, the U-Drop Inn fell into disrepair with the decommissioning of Route 66. It closed for business in the late 1990s. After it was listed on the National Register of Historic Places in September 1997, the building was purchased by the First National Bank of Shamrock, which then gave it to the city. Primarily funded by a US$1.7 million federal grant, the city hired a firm specializing in historical renovation to restore the building to its original glory and adapt it into a museum, visitors' centre, gift shop, and the city's chamber of commerce. In the 2006 animated film *Cars*, the fictional town of Radiator Springs was based on multiple real U.S. Route 66 landmarks from Peach Springs to Baxter Springs; the U-Drop Inn's distinctive architecture appears as Ramone's automotive body and paint shop.

I did read that Elvis himself was known to stop here for burgers when passing, and I just loved that bit of the history. The town itself is on the quiet side with not many shops open at all. I stopped by the local McDonalds as there was not really that much to offer in the town that I was happy to go too on my own as at that point the heat had made me feel a little off and just wanted to get some food and chill out in the hotel. I was staying at the Holiday inn and it was in the middle of a refurbishment but this did not bother me at all, as my room was just perfect! The TV must have been a 50 inch screen, full HD and way more channels than some of the others. As I got started on my food and the bag of junk I had I just chilled out in a beautiful armchair watching shows and I was really enjoying my time now, of course I missed my family but I had gotten into the swing of it now and I always had an episode of the Simpsons in the back of my mind with Bart saying "day times are awesome, night times are scary"

I was loving my time here and feeling full up, I finished my huge cup of ice cold Pepsi and went to bed.

Texas (Day 5)

I was woken by my alarm at 6am, the little noise of the air con going in the background. I did the usual video call home and was able to figure out the hot drink machine to make a cup of tea, my first since the airplane. I sat in the big arm chair with my feet up and drank the tea looking over my plans for the day, and today was going to be the best day on my trip!
Today I was meeting my cousin Kent for the very first time.
After a nice shower I packed a bag of the free goodies from the bathroom they give you and made my way down to breakfast. This hotel was just amazing not only was my room great, but the option for breakfast was good too. I never had the sausage and eggs as I was planning a big lunch with Kent. Around 7.30am I made my way outside to do some filming and it was already really hot. I wanted to see the Blarney stone as this was a little must see for my half Irish side and kissing it for good luck was a very welcome thing for the rest of my trip. Now there is a discrepancy with the Blarney stone as there are two of them in the town of Shamrock and no one actually knows what the real one is so I thought id kiss both.
I found the first stone with no issues at all did some filming and gave it a kiss, and in the back of my mind

with the thousands of travellers on the mother road I did wonder if this could have been ground zero for covid-19. I gave a little wipe with my hand like it would actually make a difference, and kissed the stone. I could feel the luck go though me, or should say I told myself I was going to be lucky as fuck from now on.

I got back into Chevy Chev my hire car and headed back onto Route 66 and as I drove along I noticed again on my trip the amount of shops that were closed down. Now there must have been 30 in say 100 meters of road all closed broken windows and boarded doors. Now depending on whom you talk to in the towns along Route 66 you will hear that the shops closed due to covid-19 and that the towns were already on their way out and covid had nothing to do with it.

As I drove towards my next stop I saw what is called "The leaning tower of Texas" or "The leaning tower of Britten" which happens to be written around the top so let's go with that one for now.

 The **Leaning Tower of Britten** is a leaning water tower which serves as a roadside attraction and decorative item along historic U.S. Route 66 in Groom, Texas. Sometimes called the Leaning Tower of Texas, the tower was originally a functioning water tower which was slated for demolition until Ralph Britten purchased and moved it to serve as an advertisement for his truck stop and tourist information centre. The Leaning Tower Truck Stop closed in the mid 1980s after it was damaged by an electrical fire; a small remaining portion operates as a local truck repair shop.

Deliberately leaning at a roughly 10 degree angle, the tower is a popular tourist destination. There is a small gravel road on the site for parking and taking pictures. During the Christmas season, the city of Groom places a large multicoloured star on top of the tower. Images of the water tower are common in Route 66 photography books, just like this one.

The heat was not getting to me at this point however it was still early on in the day and I had a very long drive ahead, so after a little filming and a photo from different angles I was back on the road.

I was now in Amarillo Texas and my stop here would be a HUGE Walmart.

This was great I walked around looking at everything they had, from pain killers, bulk soft drinks to shot guns.

I brought some cream for a bite I had from before my trip that was now really getting to me, the Jungle formula I brought was not touching it, but the cream I did buy that I've never seen or heard of before Chiggerex. Now this stuff worked on the spot and I only had to use it once! I stocked up on Pepsi and junk food for the night, as well as sweets to bring back home and at last, a sat nav.

The plan was to only use this if I really got in the shit as I could not use it when I got back to the UK, and I had done ok over the last 4 days.

I headed down to a town called Lubbock to meet my cousin Kent who was going to meet me half way and we agreed on my choice of venue, Hooters.

When in Rome an all that I thought I'd make a point of going in a Hooters as I had never been on one and I was on holiday, my adventure and it turned out to be a great choice.

It was a 2 hour drive to Lubbock and the heat was unreal! The air con was on full and when I touched the side window it was hot to the touch, this was real Texas. Even with the air con on full blast it was baking in the car and I was dripping in sweat and started to feel very unwell. I pulled over and remembered the water George had let me take back in Gary's gay parita; I drank both bottles and felt better right away. The Pepsi I had was just making me feel worse but that water helped me no end, I can't thank George enough. I carried on driving making a mental note that no matter how expensive the water is I was buying it!

As I drove I passed what looked like the longest train in the world, I could see cattle farms and miles of wind turbines and that was about it, the road was straight.

I put my foot down to make sure I was on time not realising that the road had gone from 75mph to 60mph due to some roadwork's ahead.

The only bend on the road I went round happened to have a police car sitting there with a speed gun, so I looked down and made sure I was doing bang on 75mph. I can't begin to tell you how fast this police officer turned round and was pulling me over, I actually thought he was going to pass me but nope, I was in the shit!
I stopped the car and opened the window and the rush of heat hit me like a hair dryer. This police officer sat behind me in his car for a while then took a slow walk to me. I was expecting "licence and registration" like you see in the films, but he just said "do you know how fast you were going?"
I wanted to reply "well it depends on how far you have been following me" but my balls were somewhere in my belly and my arsehole was tighter than a used honey jar at the back of a kitchen cupboard.
I said "75" I knew it was 75mph as I saw him before his gun could of picked me up.
The officer replied "you're not from round here then" and before I could say anything I remembered the film Deliverance and thought I could hear a banjo.
I explained what I was doing and going and he was just about to write me a ticket then said "well I better get the car back as it must have a fault, no way was you speeding in this piece of shit" put his book away and walked away laughing. I just sat there in case he was not done with me, but he drove off and even gave a wave. I could not get the window up fast enough and the air con

back on. I looked at the temp on the car dash which said 103, which is around 39 to us in the UK.

Soon enough I was in Lubbock and almost out of petrol, but I made it I was at Hooters.

As I walked inside the air con was like a give from the gods it was perfect.

Kent had already made it and was sitting down, It was so good to see him in person and we chatted away. I ordered a BBQ bacon burger meal and I have to say it was one of the best burgers I had while I was in the USA. The service was outstanding and it was nothing like I thought it would be, maybe as it was lunch time but it was quiet. Our waitress kept filling my huge coke glass up and we had a great chat and it turned out her boyfriend was from Bristol which is not that far from me back home.

Kent arranged a group photo for me and then we were able to get a photo together. Kent had brought me lots of birthday presents which made me feel really loved as this was something I was not used to back home. We only spent a short time together but we really got on. Now what I was not aware of was the communication going on behind the scenes. Kent had been in contact with my other cousins Sharon and Michelle who were keeping tabs on my trip making sure I was ok. They had spoken to Kent and told him about my water situation and he had got a large case of bottled water for me. This was perfect!

It was then I felt a cousins love, growing up it was really just me and my mum so this was alien to me but I was not going to reject it, but grab it with open arms. Kent showed me his guns which I thought was amazing as Texas is what is called "an open carry state" meaning you can walk around with a gun on your side. Kent even had a Jeep Wrangler which happens to be my dream car, I had a cool cousin.

We said our goodbyes and I was back on the road, making a quick stop to fill the petrol tank. By the time I made it back to Amarillo and got back on Route 66 I was tired, but seeing the route 66 signs got me back in the game. I made my way to Cadillac Ranch and this was another must see on my to do list. My sat nav took me thought real Texas country, ranches and just miles of nothing. I soon found a little stop called the 2nd amendment cowboy RV Park, I later found out it's also the gift shop for the Cadillac ranch which I missed out on. It was now 113 on the car dash which is 45 to us in the UK.

It turns out June is one of the hottest months in the USA and the locals told me it was one of the hottest they had had in many years, and just my luck the time I chose to do the trip.

After taking a quick photo I was back in the car and maybe a mile up the road I made it!

I parked up and made my way into the ranch, they had a trailer that sold spray paint at of course way over price.

I brought a black and white can and made my way to the Cadillac's.

Cadillac Ranch is a public art installation and sculpture in Amarillo, Texas, US. It was created in 1974 by Chip Lord, Hudson Marquez and Doug Michel's, who were a part of the art group Ant Farm.
The installation consists of ten Cadillac's (1949–1963) buried nose-first in the ground. Installed in 1974, the cars were either older running, used or junk cars — together spanning the successive generations of the car line — and the defining evolution of their tailfins. The cars are inclined at the same angle as the pyramids at Giza.
It's a fun little attraction that comes with free parking and is free to enter so paying a little more for spray paint on site was ok. But I didn't actually need to buy any at all, as when you get close to the cars the whole area is littered with plastic lids and spray cans. The litter bins were almost empty and it was such a sad sight that everyone was just throwing the cans on the ground. There was a real strong wind that was like a strong hot air hitting me no stop, the wind did not let up at all. I did what I could do in the wind with the spray cans but it was just too strong to really do some art work. I walked back to the car giving one last look on my shoulder before getting in the car and getting back on the mother road.

I drove another 40 odd miles and made it to the Midpoint café. Along with everything else on route 66 it closed at 4pm and I missed it by seconds. It was mainly the midpoint line I was here for. I was now exactly half way through my trip, this would have been better doing it with someone but I needed to do this trip alone, I was learning more and more about myself each day pushing myself to my limits and at this point the fear had gone. Before and leaving Chicago I was scared a little of what could and would happen on my trip but now I had hardened up to it all. It made me think of Tom Hanks in the movie Big where he checks into the St James hotel and is scared then later on you see him just getting on with it.

Now planning a route 66 trip is so much harder than it should be, I just put down what I wanted to see and not what the guide books tell you to see. There's a huge driving distance between most of the stops and everything closes at around 4pm so a lot of things were closed by the time I made it and after talking to a few Brits on the route they said they too felt the same as things were closed. So it's ideal to research the route and see what you really want to see and what you don't mind missing out on just in case.

The drive to the hotel was a hard one; the side wind was like nothing I'd ever experienced before even as a coach driver back in the UK.

It started to ease off as I got into New Mexico which I was thankful for.

As I made it into Tucumcari along route 66 it was again a long road of broken dreams closed motels, closed shops and the building were decaying, paint hanging off the walls, this was the real America. I pulled into the Blue Swallow Motel which was going to be my stop for the night and one of the two hotels I had to book 8 months in advance for.

The story of the Blue Swallow Motel began when Carpenter W.A. Huggins purchased lots on March 29th, 1939 and began construction.

The Blue Swallow Court, as it was originally called, was open and operating with ten rooms sometime in 1940. Mr. and Mrs. Huggins operated both the motor court and a cafe on the site. Ted Jones, a prominent eastern New Mexico rancher, was the first long-term owner/operator. Facing Route 66, the Blue Swallow offers access to motorists from both the highway and a side street. The motel has an L-shaped plan and consists of 12 units (two more were added by approximately 1948) with a centrally-located office and manager's residence. Garage units, some with original wood overhead doors, are located between the sleeping units. With its pink stucco walls decorated with shell designs and a stepped parapet, the façade reflects a modest use of the Southwest Vernacular style of architecture. When Mr. Jones and his wife died in the 1950s, Lillian Redman and her husband bought the Blue Swallow and successfully operated it, modernizing by installing a new, larger neon sign, and using the more up-to-date term, "Motel". From the start, the Redman's put their customers first. When guests didn't have enough money for a room, the Redman's accepted personal belongings in trade or provided the room for free. Ms. Redman and the Blue Swallow became icons of Route 66 folklore. She described the special and close connection she had with the Route 66 motorists who came in each night this way. "I end up travelling the highway in my heart with whoever stops here for the night."

At the end of the 1960s, Interstate 40, a faster, limited-access highway, took the place of the old Route 66. The development of this new highway drastically changed the traffic circulation of Route 66 affecting many of the businesses along the way, including the Blue Swallow Motel. Ms. Redman said of the effect of Interstate 40, which bypassed Tucumcari, "When Route 66 was closed to the majority of traffic and the other highway came in, I felt just like I had lost an old friend. But some of us stuck it out and are still here on Route 66." After owning the Blue Swallow for almost 40 years, Ms. Redman sold the motel in the late 1990s. Extensive restoration work was performed by owners Dale and Hilda Bakke, modernizing electrical systems and repairing neon, installing 1939 Bell rotary-dial phones in each room, while retaining all of the historic character and charm of the Blue Swallow. Bill and Terri Kinder purchased the Blue Swallow in 2006, selling it to Kevin and Nancy Mueller in 2011. The Mueller family is credited with creating the Lillian Redman Suite, updating the structure of rooms, reinforcing flooring, updating plumbing and providing modern conveniences. Robert and Dawn Federico purchased the Blue Swallow Motel in June 2020, and will continue to preserve and protect the motel's legacy.

The Motel was listed on the National Register of Historic Places in 1993. There is a plethora of information available about the Blue Swallow online as well as in various publications and books. It was an easy choice to stay here, the history alone was worth it not to mention the ghost stories of Lillian Redman herself checking in on the guests wanting to make sure everyone was happy.
When Lillian ran the Blue Swallow Motel, each guest was provided with a copy of this benediction. A printed copy is in each room today.
I got to the check in and gift shop area and was met by Rob and Dawn the current owners of the Blue Swallow who I had heard were very welcoming but they turned out to be the best Motel hosts on the route. We got talking and I was shown my room and given the history of it, even with a new TV on the wall and mattress etc everything else was original to the hotel from when it

opened. It was like stepping back in time but with today's modern comforts. I was told I could park in what was an original parking space under a shelter right next to my room which was perfect for Chevy Chev.

I got my bags in and went back to the check in to buy some gifts and bits for me such as a T-shirt and a room 4 key ring which I have to say is a nice touch to have. Rob then said "we have PG tips, help yourself to a tea" They had thought of everything! I had a tea then got back in the car to fill up with petrol ready for the next day and find some food. I asked a local girl working in the gas station wheres the best place to get a hot meal was and she recommended Sonic as I didn't want to sit in a restaurant as such on my own. I'd never heard of it before but it's a huge chain in the USA and it was only across the road. I had a chilli cheese dog and fries and lemonade. Now if you ever go to the USA get lemonade it's nothing like we have in the UK and every place was different in taste, Sonic was outstanding.

I made my way back to the motel, filled up my ice bucket and made a start on the fizzy drinks I had brought from pop's soda ranch. I have to say they are nothing to write home about at all I actually found some to be more watery and lacking any real flavour, the cola was nice but that was about it.

The motel has a seating area outside every room and seems to have everyone at night sitting outside drinking and chatting away about the trip they are on, some were doing route 66 heading towards Chicago so we gave each other little tips on hotels and places to see. Rob and Dawn lived on site and their home was directly opposite and said if I needed anything at all give them a knock. That's a big deal in my book and I'm going to make a point of staying here again whatever the cost, I felt looked after here! My room was number 4 and I was happy about this as A YouTuber had stayed in this very room I was in and did a video so it was cool to watch the video about the room I was inside of.

I got into the most comfortable bed ever; it felt so good laying there, cold drink in hand and watching the TV.

I'm so happy I got to stay at the Blue Swallow Motel; it lived up to its reputation and some! The benediction on the wall of each read as follows.

Greetings Traveler:

In ancient times, there was a prayer for "The Stranger Within our Gates." Because this motel is a human institution to serve people, and not solely a money-making organization, we hope that God will grant you peace and rest while you are under our roof.

May this room and motel be your "second" home. May those you love be near you in thoughts and dreams. Even though we may not get to know you, we hope that you will be as comfortable and happy as if you were in your own house.

May the business that brought you this way prosper. May every call you make and every message you receive add to your joy. When you leave, may your journey be safe. We are all travellers. From "birth till death," we travel between the eternities. May these days be pleasant for you, profitable for society, helpful for those you meet, and a joy to those you know and love best.

Sincerely yours, Lillian Redman (owner of the Blue Swallow Motel from 1958-1998)

I wish I got to meet Lillian and maybe I did and just didn't know?

New Mexico (Day 6)

What a great night's sleep! I was fully recharged and ready to see a place I've wanted to see for many many years!
The Tinkertown museum! This was not on or even close to route 66 but I just had to come and see it for myself. It was 160 miles from the Blue Swallow and a drive north of route 66 to a area called Sandia Crest.
I had no signal at all on my phone but I was able to find it. The museum is hidden away in the mountains and when I pulled up I was so excited I was like a kid in a toy shop.
It cost me $6 to get in but id of been happy to pay five times the amount. I had a pocket of quarters and I was given two more on my way in and the lady who sold me the ticket said "the first two are on us". They have little attractions around the site that when you put a quarter in you can watch vintage toys move and play music. Id waited 5 years to see this place in person, after seeing it on TV and videos online. For those who don't know or have heard of this place here's a little back story.
It took Ross Ward over 40 years to carve, collect, and lovingly construct what is now Tinkertown Museum. His miniature wood-carved figures were first part of a travelling exhibit, driven to county fairs and carnivals in the 1960s and '70s. Today over 50,000 glass bottles form rambling walls that surround a 22-room museum.

Wagon wheels, old fashioned store fronts, and wacky western memorabilia make Tinkertown's exterior as much as a museum as the wonders within.

Inside, the magic of animation takes over. The inhabitants of a raucous little western town animate to hilarious life. Under the big top, diminutive circus performers challenge tigers and defy gravity while the Fat Lady fans herself and a polar bear teeters and totters. Throughout, eccentric collections of Americana (wedding cake couples, antique tools, bullet pencils and much, much more) fill Tinkertown's winding hallways. Otto the one-man-band and Esmeralda, the Fortune Teller, need only a quarter to play a tune or predict your future. Through a doorway and across a ramp waits a big-sized surprise: a 35′ antique wooden sailboat that braved a 10 year voyage around the world.

I first saw Tinkertown on an Adam the woo video via his channel on YouTube, and actually being here was so unreal!

I took my time walking around looking at the models and taking in every single detail of the houses and what's going on inside them, the detail was perfect and would have taken hundreds of hours each to make. In the middle of the museum I bumped into two sisters from Manchester who were also doing route 66 and had a good chat. After saying our good lucks, I carried on and was in an area where they had vintage toys from India and other places from around the world.

One of the best that I saw was a side show set that had so much to see it took me ages to really take it all in, it is so unique here. I wish I could go see it again right now as I write this, and I really wish it well. Everyone must see this place, and I can't wait to go back.

On my way out I bumped into the lady who sold me the ticket just as I was coming out of the gift shop with my bag of goodies and we had a really good talk. She took so much interest in me and my trip, and I listened to how the museum is run and the history. She gave me a big hug before I left and it was very welcome. We said bye and I was back on the road and I was heading into Albuquerque to see the Breaking Bad filming locations. My first stop was Walter white's house; I could not believe I was here. I can recall wanting to see the locations and I was finally here doing it. The house was gated off and even after all these years since the show finished it was still very busy with fans taking photos. From there I went to the Jessie Pinkman house which seemed to have a lot of dodgy looking people walking around and for what looks like a very posh and expensive area it just did not feel that safe. From there I headed to the carwash that is used at the start of the show and the final seasons, and it was packed I was going to treat Chevy Chev to a wash but the line of cars was just to long for me to wait as I had a major drive ahead. The building used for Los Pollos Hermanos is called Twister, I was going to go inside but the area was run down and I was getting a lot of looks from a large group of guys wondering if I was filming them or the building. It was now time for lunch and I had one place in mind, "The Dog House". One of the oldest drive thru places in the area used in 3 or 4 different episodes of Breaking Bad and the birth place of the chilli cheese dog. I pulled in and my order was taken at the car, I ordered a chilli cheese dog with onions, paid and waited. The food was delivered quick and I got stuck in, now they did forget the onions but it was not a big deal at all. The hotdogs themselves were very skinny and long and there were two in the bun. It tasted so good, a little spicy but it was everything I thought it would be. This was the first meal that I had some balls behind me other that the salad I had at pop's soda ranch. I took the risk of shitting up my back for the sake of eating a chilli dog at the home of the very first one.

It was time for a very long dive to my next hotel and id be taking one of the longest stretches of the mother road. The 136 mile drive took longer than I thought due to the tight turns and the need to stop to take it all in. I was able to find Owl rock, it's called this due to it looking like an own sitting down. I had seen this in a few books and when doing research online I did see a number of people had missed it while driving through. This part of the mother road is mainly through the New Mexico desert with little towns along the way. I was really here doing the route 66 that I grew up watching, the dirt and dust roads linking the East to the West.

I carried on till I hit my final stop of the day, Gallup New Mexico home to the world famous El Rancho motel.

It was such a beautiful building oozing history, the car park was filled with Harley Davidson's and bikers walking around but they said hello to me on my way inside to check in, everyone was having a fun time.

As you enter the historic El Rancho through the stately front entry, you immediately realize this was and still is a special place….During its heyday, the El Rancho Hotel was one of the premier hotels in the entire Southwest and became the place for the Hollywood set to stay when filming in the area.

During its glory years, the El Rancho was the definition of luxury and included many amenities that were lacking in other typical tourist hotels of the day.

For 50 years, the El Rancho Hotel greeted guests along Route 66 with class and dignity. Luckily for us, this one-of-a-kind hotel once again greets guests with open arms and enjoys the renewed worldwide interest in Route 66 and its landmarks.

Most of if not all of the rooms here had had an actor stay in them, this was the place to be.

I got my key and made my way to room 305 Sidney Greenstreet room. I put my case in the room and went for a walk around the hotel, I felt quite lonely as I walked around, and ended up spending an hour going between the lobby and first floor seating area just sitting there people watching as it made me feel less on my own. They have display cabinets filled with items belonging to the legend himself John Wayne; it was strange looking at his cowboy hat looking at all the little bits of dirt, marks and sweat.

I went down to the restaurant and had a burger for my dinner and headed back to my room. I watched TV for a few hours then fell asleep and was in a deep sleep till I heard a loud bang on the door of my room, I got out of bed and as I walked to the door half asleep I thought I was about to bump into a girl I even moved to the side and said "sorry love". I opened the door and it was quiet, I can't see anyone playing any games with me but you can never tell. As I got into bed I remembered the girl I had just seen so I got up turned on all the lights and looked around before going back to sleep.

At around 4.30am I woke up by someone calling my name, I put this down to a dream and went back to sleep but it happened again around 6am and this time I just stayed up and got ready for another day on the mother road.

Arizona (Day 7)

I came down to check out like I had at all the other hotels and had become quite the hotel/motel connoisseur at this point, however this checkout was different.
The young girl "Maria" who was checking me out looked at my room key and then said "was everything ok with your room?"
I said yes but then remembered the bang on the door and mentioned it not in a complaint way but just brought it up as she had asked.
I was then informed that the room I had stayed in was in fact one of the most haunted room in the hotel and the room was featured on an episode of Ghost Adventures. How did I miss this episode? I'm a huge fan of the show and somehow missed out on this one. It was only when I got back to the UK that I was able to watch the episode and saw my room on it. Was I half asleep and maybe still in a dream when I saw the girl in my room? Or did I in fact come face to face with one of the spirits that are said to be seen by guests in the hotel? I don't think we will ever know but I'm so happy I got to stay in the room used on the TV show even if I got to see it after.
When I got out to the car park I noticed a lot of homeless People asking for loose change, so I made a point of not doing any filming outside as it made me feel uneasy.
I drove for an hour and stopped off at a Denny's in Holbrook, and looking back now it was definitely a great

chose as since I've read that the Denny's chain has closed down. I had a huge breakfast here and the staff were amazing, this was something I really liked in the USA you get a great service at every stop.

I only had one main stop today I wanted to see the jack Rabbit trading post, and see the world famous "Here it is" sign that's been a staple on Route 66 for many many years.

In 1949 Jim Taylor bought a building in Arizona on Route 66. On the move here he had a statue of a black rabbit in the back of a convertible car. Along the way people kept saying they liked it & took lots of pics of it. So when he got here he put it in the ground so people could sit on it & take pics. That was how the Jack Rabbit Trading Post was born. That rabbit eventually became the model for the "HERE IT IS" sign & the famous mileage signs that you have heard about. Jim Taylor owned the store but leased it much of the time he had it.

Glenn Blansett leases it in 1961 & bought it in 1967. In 1969 his son Phil & daughter-in-law Pat bought the business. Their daughter & son-in-law Cindy & Tony Jaquez, who still own and operate, bought the store in 1995.

Now this place is Amazing and one thing that I really wanted to buy was a mileage sign.

It's a yellow metal sign and you have the miles from your home to the store, and it was a must buy on my list. I had no signal on my phone and the store internet was down and I was worried that I would not be able to have one made but the owner Cindy called her son at work and got him to look up the mileage for us.

They got the number and had the sign made while I walked around the store picking up gifts to take home.

I got back to the till with a big basket of items and Tony handed me the sign, as I looked at it I saw the number **5094** and my stomach went over, it was at this point that it hit me just how far I was away from my family, and the further West I drove the higher the number was going to be.

Cindy took my photo outside with me holding the sign for their Facebook page and I was over the moon as I was not in any photo up until this point as I was alone, so it was nice to have a photo.

I got back on the mother road and my next stop of the day was Winslow AZ.

As I drove I noticed a lot of signs along the way advertising if anyone thinks they witness sex trafficking to call 911.

Now for the amount of signs for Human Trafficking, and to look out for young girls who have been sex trafficked it must be an issue here, and I thought about the two sisters I met back in Tinkertown who were doing the route together and hoped they would be ok. This was something that I'm well aware of as I've seen it on TV and films but to actually see signs along the major highways made me feel uneasy.

I made it to Winslow and parked up, they have an area that is a major tourist attraction after the song "take it easy" by the eagles. Now the song was written in Flagstaff a little further up the road but it was nice to see a statue of the band and a flat bed Ford truck that you could look at and take photos. I never stood around too long as the heat was really bad and it was a very hot and dry heat, so I made my way into the gift shop on the opposite corner and was met with huge prices and amazing air con.

The average price for a magnet and key ring was around $18.00 and most of the shops along the route sold the same items and the odd town names with route 66 printed on it. I did get myself a key ring and a magnet here to take home and I made my way back to the car. Maybe a mix of the heat and long days but I was so tired at this point and I just sat in the car for a while watching the other tourists, and families together, I longed for a chat with someone, all these years I had planned to do this trip on my own my big adventure travelling America but I had never thought about how I would feel. In hindsight it was the most selfish thing I've ever done and I missed my family.

On my way out of Winslow I had to stop the car and double check what I thought I had seen.

It was a Wilts and Dorset double Decker bus, and I had actually worked for Wilts and Dorset the year before my trip so seeing this bus just sat in the desert was sad to see it all broken but cheered me up as it was something from home.

I carried on to Flagstaff and parked up, it was only $1 an hour to park which I thought was amazing as Flagstaff is a huge tourist area and was very busy. The streets were filled with local shops, and the pavements were packed with people. It was not a place that was on my must see but it was good to walk around for while. I found the Hotel Monte vista which Michael J Fox has stayed in many times when passing through, and the hotel sign on the roof was a stop off for many people to take photos at night as it boasted huge yellow neon lights that looked outstanding at night.

I was on too much of a time sensitive trip at this point so I just looked around for a while and took a slow walk back to the car. I drove to the next town Williams and that would be my home for the night.

I checked into the Lodge on 66 and it was the first real Motel that I had stayed in that I could park outside my room like in the films, this did worry me a little but the town of Williams was beautiful and one of the biggest on the Route. I was in room 11 "Shamrock" it was a small room but very nice. I asked in the reception what the best things were to see and she explained what was in the town then mentioned that the Grand Canyon was an hour's drive North of Williams so it was a no brainer for me; I was going to see the Grand Canyon. On my way up I stopped at a Wendy's in Tusayan for a late lunch and rest as the road was long and the heat was really getting to me. As I sat in Wendy's I looked around and it was all families and I hoped someone would talk to me or maybe see some of the other Brits on the route that I had seen before, but no such luck. I finished my meal and took my huge Wendy's cup that I had just got and carried on to the Grand Canyon.

I finally arrived at the main gates where you pay to get in, I thought it was free to see but it's being looked after by a national parks company. It cost me $35 to get in and they don't take cash!

At first I thought it was expensive but it turns out the $35.00 ticket was actually a 7 day pass for me and the car to get in, I was only going to go the once but it's a great deal as back in the UK you would pay more for a national trust site and can only go once. After the payment gates I headed to **Mather Point,** which is a look out area of the Canyon and a little less busy than the other areas. If you are coming to the Grand Canyon from Williams this is the most direct part and the quickest to get too, there are a few petrol stations on the way up but I recommend filling up in Williams as I found it a little cheaper than the stations on the way.

I got to the Mather point car park and it was cooler here which was better for me but it was still a hot day. I started to feel out of breath as I walked up so I took my time. As I got to the top of a long path I saw it, I was here! The Grand Canyon!

It looked like a screen saver I've never seen anything like it I just stood there looking out, at it trying to take it all in, I looked to my left and noticed everyone walking along another path to what looked like a better area with a viewing area. I made my way along breathing in the fresh air and looking out over the Canyon, I just could not believe I was here, it was absolutely beautiful.

I sat down In the Mather point Amphitheatre which is made from native stone and built to be a seating area along the south rim of the Grand Canyon.

I watched a guy get down on one knee and propose to his girlfriend, I've never seen this happen before. Everyone including myself gave a clap and cheer, and again was looking out at the natural beauty. Before I knew it I was sitting alone I had not even noticed that everyone had moved on. I missed my family so much at this point and wanted them here with me to see what I was seeing, to share it with me. But I was on a mission and an adventure, and I would see them soon enough. I took loads of photos and videos then headed back to Williams. I was around 20 miles outside of Williams and I noticed to my right a big Flintstones sign with Fred on it, so I pulled into a parking area, this was the old

Bedrock city attraction. I had seen this on YouTube a few times but never knew where it was.

Bedrock City is a Flintstones-themed roadside attraction consisting of an amusement park and RV park at the corner of Arizona State Route 64 and U.S. Route 180 in Coconino County, in the U.S. state of Arizona. The park was opened in 1972, following the owners' success with a predecessor park near Mount Rushmore in South Dakota. The park licenses the likenesses of the Flintstones characters, and features statues, rides, and a diner based on that theme.

In 2015, the park's owner, Linda Speckles, was planning to retire and sell the park for $2 million US. The park was closed on January 28, 2019, but reopened in mid-June and remained open through the end of summer 2019. As of the location's 50th anniversary in 2022, it has been incorporated as part of the Raptor Ranch conservation park, with plans to remain open "indefinitely."

The RV part was still open and had a huge shop/gift shop on site that was still running. It looked like it was being changed to something else, but I was so happy I got to see the original signage and see a few items that had been left over. It's amazing what you can see and find out of the blue on a road trip. I made it back to the motel and took a walk around Williams. This was a busy little town all the shops were packed and I went in one of the gift shops which had the world's biggest metal Route

66 sign. The bars were packed and everyone was having a great time. I went to my room and relaxed and went over everything I was going to do the next day and use my Booking.com app on my phone to book the next night's hotel. This was the first day that I had really felt a true Route 66 experience, and it was only going to get better from now on, I was in true West America now and everything seemed to feel more route 66 if that's a word? It felt and looked more like the films and things you see on TV.

Las Vegas (day 8)

This was a VERY long night, the bed was not great at all as I lay down my legs were in the air I had a car park light coming in the room that I could not stop and all the draws in the room were open in the morning. This morning I was going to have breakfast at the motel to try save some money, and get my money's worth.
I filled up my huge Wendy's cup from the day before with ice at the hotel, and filled it with a bottle of Pepsi I had brought. This was a much cheaper option on the route as drinks were expensive.
I filled the car up with petrol and headed to Seligman, this is a VERY important town to see on Route 66, it's the town Disney Car's was based on and the home to Angel Delgadillo, the man who saved Route 66 from disappearing forever. Angel's barber shop is still here in the town but now only open for those on the mother road can come by and see. The Snowcap is the most famous in the town and was once owned by Angel's late brother. I wanted to get one of their famous hotdogs that I had read so much about but it was closed on the day I was in the town, due to illness the day before. I was told by staff in the gift shop next door that it was going to be open a little later on but I decided to give it a miss and carry on my way, I did really want to try the hotdog and only had to wait an hour but for some reason I wanted to just get back on the road again. I

took loads of photos around the town and wondered what it was like for those who lived here?

There is a bar in the town that I had been told to stay away from as it was a real rough place, but I did make a point of going to see it.

I got in Chevy Chev and headed along Route 66 to Kingman, and even though it was going to take longer I made a point of staying away from the I40 and stayed on the old Route 66 even with its bad bumpy roads, this is what I was here to do and I was going to do it.

I pulled Chevy Chev over to the side of the road between Antares and Hualapal and just looked around, desert for miles, no cars either way I was fully alone just me and the mother road, complete silence!

The years of hurt, sadness, anger being let down all came out and I just stood in the middle of the mother road and cried. I had finally found myself; I knew who I was and even writing this down now has given me a lump in my throat. I was free; I just stood in the middle of the road looking around slowly trying to catch my breath then out of nowhere I let out a loud scream. It felt so good to just get it all out, and I felt better. I sat on the bonnet of Chevy Chev drinking an ice cold beer while staring along the mother road thinking of the millions who have taken this pilgrimage before me, and the millions after. I've never felt so alive; I jumped back in the car and headed to Kingman. As I drove down the mother road I think it was a gofer ran out in front of the car and I killed it, it absolutely broke my heart that I could do nothing. I've never worked out why this happened to me I just hope it was over quick, this was something that would be etched into my memories for the rest of my life.

A little further up the road I came across an abandoned bar called "Bert's country dancing". It was all boarded up but I stood and thought about the history of this place, maybe fellow Route 66 pilgrims stopped off here for a drink and a dance? Maybe someone got engaged here? I took some photos and carried on to Kingman.

Kingman was baking hot and I quickly made my way inside the visitor centre for the air con and to get my passport stamped. As I came out I walked across the road to look at a vintage steam train and as I walked back to the car I could not believe my eyes, it was Terry and Jerry! It was so good to see these guys again, and it really was an honour to meet them.

We had a good chat about the things we had seen and how we felt about the trip and I can't begin to tell you how happy I was to see the twins but I knew it would be the last time id see them. They had plans for their birthday to spend some time in Las Vegas and I would be a few towns ahead by then, so I'm grateful for the time I spent with them. We had a chat and did some filming at Mr D's diner then said our goodbyes. It was sad walking away but I'm hopeful that ill see them again one day. The twins told me they were going to see the Hoover dam and I had no idea at all how close it was to us so I decided to stop off for some photos on the way to Las Vegas.

The Hoover dam was packed with visitors and it had a line of cars going into the car park, but thanks to YouTube I knew where I could stop for a little while and not pay for the parking.
If I ever go back I think I'd take the dam tour and spend a few hours here but I just wanted to get to Vegas as the heat was getting to me and I wanted a shower and relax, so I just took some photos, did some filming and I was back on the road to Vegas.
The drive took ages as I got caught in rush hour traffic, and this was the first real traffic I had been in since I got to America and coming from London I thought I'd seen it all but this was 5 solid lanes.
I finally got to the hotel, I had booked a room at the Hilton World resort and the building was huge. It had a few hotels a casino, and shopping units all in the same building. This looked like it had been designed so you never have to leave it was all under one roof.
It took me ages to get checked in and get to my room but it was worth the wait. The room was huge boasting a 60 inch screen TV with everything I could want to watch, free water in the fridge and one of the best queen size beds I've ever been on. What I never saw was a waited mini bar area, that sold phone cables, and very expensive wines, nuts and the usual suspects you find in hotels. I found this by putting

my bag down and knocking it all over which started a timer so I spend a few seconds just looking at this count down and reading the laminated sheet that explained after 60 seconds anything not on the mini bar scale unit would be charged for. So I flew into action like I was on an episode of the Cube standing everything back up. I had seconds to spare but it lit up green again and all was good with the mini bar again. I put my bag on the bed while laughing and taking a mental note to make sure I never make this mistake again! By this time I was wide awake so I made a few calls to the Zac Bagan's haunted museum and I was able to swap my ticket from the following morning to that night. I was so excited to actually see this place; I got in the car and headed down. I'm not going to go into too much detail about the museum but I highly recommend it and I strongly advise you get the R.I.P pass, you get a free t-shirt and get to see extra stuff. In my private life I've been a paranormal researcher for over 22 years and not much shocks me, but the things I saw here could have turned me gray. I can't wait to go again!

I went back to the hotel via the Las Vegas sign and got into a long line to take a photo of the sign and I was able to do a deal with the family behind that they take my photo at the sign and I take there's, this worked out great for me. Back at the hotel I hit the casino and the aim was to spend $20 on Black at the roulette table. It turned out the minimum bet was $25, so I did that. I handed them the money and put my chip on the Black, and within 30 seconds it hit Green zero. I just smiled and walked away and got myself a few slices of pizza and went to my room.

Vegas was the most expensive place on my trip as I found myself paying $10 for a 500ml bottle of coke, everyone was out to get as much money from you as they can here, and you need real deep pockets to buy anything at all here. I went back to my room and watched Ghost Adventures on the TV while eating and drinking food and drink I almost had to take a mortgage on, but I was on an adventure and nothing was going to dampen my time.

This is going to be a short chapter as I've decided to go with the "what happens in Vegas stays in Vegas".

Oatman (day 9)

I had a good night's sleep and was up nice and early ready for an hour on the gun range. I checked out of the hotel and took a slow walk to the car as I wanted to take in the atmosphere of the Casino one last time before I headed off. I had been told about Machine Guns Vegas from a guy who had done Route 66 and had stopped off, I did a pre pay booking online back in the UK and it cost around $200.

I walked in a few hours early and was able to go right in but I fell into the trap at the desk with the offer of "extra" guns and ammo. I thought fuck it why not and had a chat with the young ladies on the desk who talked me through what I could get and the better deal. I was then introduced to a guy called Brian who was a total legend!

He took me through to the gun range and got me ready. The first gun was a 9mm Glock with 10 rounds, I took my time firing the gun and I actually did well, the second gun was a full auto and I was amazed with this one, it was like I was in a film I actually remember thinking of Robocop when he's shooting on the gun range.

Brian changed the target sheet and I started on the bigger of the guns, an M4.

This gun was heavy and I'm told its used by the American military, I did real well with this one, but it was time to swap the good guys guns and change to the bad guys gun the AK47.

I could feel the heat coming off the bullets; I was so happy that I was able to do this while in America.

I said bye to Brian and headed to Oatman to see the cowboys and donkeys.

I headed through the Mohave Desert and this must have been the hottest day by far! I was drinking bottle after bottle of water, and even the water that had been in the fridge over night and was ice cold was now too warm to drink. After a few hours I made it to Oatman and had to drive around the donkeys that would just block the road.

I parked up at the top of the town and walked down just in time to see the cowboy shoot out show. They do a show in the street at noon and 2.15pm each day and its well worth getting to Oatman to see.

This show is for a children's charity and the day I was there they had raised $19,500 I gave them a nice donation as I thought the show. I've seen this show on YouTube but it was so much better seeing it in person and really getting to experience it for myself in person.

It's a comedy sketch about holding up a bank and then trying to rob each other and shooting each other "by mistake"

After I went inside the Oatman hotel and had a burger and fries with lemonade. I have to say I was disappointed as I waited a real long time to give my order then longer to receive it. The food was warm and if I'm honest I actually felt sick after eating it, but maybe this was just due to the heat.

I wrote my name and family's names on dollar bills and put them on the wall, with thousands of others that had been put on the wall by those on the mother road and people passing through, it was actually a great sight to see and I'm told there was over $100,000 on the walls and ceiling.
I went for a walk around the town and had a look around an old gold mine that was free to go inside and look around, and I went in most of the gift shops in this tiny town. It looked like it was unchanged since the 1800s and had that cowboy feel to it, and it was miles from anything so I did wonder how those that live and work here cope? Maybe the minimal life style was key here, everyone I spoke too were happy and seemed like they were living their best life. This was something I had noticed the whole trip, even the bigger towns on the mother road everyone was happy, they didn't really have mush as the shops were sometimes a little run down and the only money they would be making is by those doing Route 66, but they were genuinely happy and would do anything for you. I came across a Native American selling handmade jewellery by the side of the road, I had a look and for what they were and the fact he had handmade them all I found them to be really cheap as some must of taken him hours to make. I picked up some bits to take home and he did me a good deal, we spoke for awhile about the tribe he came from and how he makes money and I have to say he was a really nice guy. As a kid I watched the cowboy films and even had a cowboy hat and saloon doors on my bedroom, and I would always be

on the cowboy's side and cheer for them. But after talking to him and he explained that they were protecting what was there's I could see the other side of the story, in fact I was cheering for the wrong side, the Native Americans lost so much and it's made me re think these films and history I was taught at school. He gave me directions for Route 66 and told me areas I needed to be careful on, it turned out this next part of the mother road was really dangerous and had claimed many lives over the years. I know a few people I spoke too on the mother road and on forums had decided to miss out this part all together and stay on the I40, but this was the real Route 66 I wanted to see, the miles of nothing and no one I wanted to really experience this and I had enough petrol and water to make it through as long as the car was ok. If I'm honest this was a thrill for me taking on the most dangerous part of the route, and I headed off with my handmade gifts and took a slow drive. It did however turn out to be harder than I thought and I can fully understand why so many refused to drive the old trails road as I was a fart or sneeze away from driving off a cliff. As I drove round I noticed flowers piled up in areas where people had died and one part I stopped at had a marker of a guy who had died on his Harley Davidson and the more I looked the more I understood how people were crashing, the road was winding with sharp turns and all I could see was desert for miles around, not a person or petrol station in sight.

After what felt like hours I was finally out of the desert and I crossed over into California, the final state of my trip. Due to the altitude I was at California was almost a downward hill the whole way and my ears were popping like crazy!

At this point I was ready to see my family and wanted to try see them for father's day, as I had booked my trip in such a way that I was going to be in the USA over father's day and what I needed from this trip, what I had to do I had done and achieved and it was now time to get back to the reality of life.

I drove straight to San Bernardino and checked into my hotel for the night, this was a small chain hotel and I got a bad vibe from the place the second I walked in.

I put my things in my room and walked over to a "in n out burger" and I have to say the food was good. I spent the rest of the night watching TV and deciding what I wanted to see while I was here. I found the trip to be very expensive, most meals were $20 a go then drinks and bits while I was out and about I was spending over $100 a day then I had petrol on top.

At this point I had another week till my flight home and money was going to be a struggle, so I made a point of only seeing what I really wanted too and not what I was supposed to see as I was on the route.

California (Day 10)

After what felt a bad night's sleep I was wide awake laying in bed knowing that today was the final stretch, this was it I had completed Route 66, the mother road, I had seen some amazing stuff, and met some of the nicest people In the world!

My thoughts were to either stay the next week and see some of LA as planned or get a earlier flight home the next day and be home for father's day. It was getting expensive and I was yet to receive my deposit back from the very first hotel and I had spent over $1000 that I was not expecting to pay out in hotel deposits. I've stayed in many hotels in the UK and just given a card in case of damages and mini bar charges etc, but they all wanted a credit card deposit in the USA I really wish I had checked. I made a point to eat as much as I could at the hotel so I could save some money and fit as much in as I could.

I checked out and put my case in the car, I checked the oil and water and filled up the screen wash, I was amazed at how good Chevy Chev was, she was a small car but I have to say I'd be happy to own one. From the hotel I made my way to the site of the very first ever McDonalds.

I got to the site which is now a museum which is free to go into but they do take donations, I put $6.00 in the burger money box and went in and checked it out.

You don't need to be a fan of McDonalds to check this place out its filled with every single happy meal toy ever made from every country in the world that has a restaurant. I looked around and saw things that reminded me of being a child; they even had all the food cartons from all the years that really took me back. This place is a treasure trove of memories from everyone's childhood there's something in here that everyone can relate to; it really was a trip down memory lane.

This was the last stop that I had planned for the Route 66 trip and it was now time, it was time to finish this!

On my way to the car I bumped into a family from the UK and we had a chat for a while and I'm glad I saw these guys as the first thing they said to me was "the hotels are killing my cards with the deposits".

I carried on to Chevy Chev with a smile on my face that I was not the only one who messed up by not checking.

The heat started to really kick in from getting to the McDonalds location to coming out an hour later it had gone from 20 degrees to 45 degrees, I can't ever get used to the heat in America the time I spent here it just got a little more bearable. I sat in the car with the air con on full and just sat there looking around, watching the locals just going about their normal day to day life and I thought all this would still be going on right now if I was in the UK but I'm here seeing it. Maybe it was the heat but I sat there in the car for ages looking around before I got back on the road to finish the trip.

As I got close to Santa Monica pier which was the end of the trail point I found a car park and headed in. It cost me

$25.00 for 3 hours parking and it was filled with security so it was ideal really. I was around 200 meters from the end and I was filled with emotions and thinking of all the things I had done and seen as I walked to the end. I got to the world famous Santa Monica pier sign and just stopped and looked and I could not believe I was actually here.

I walked down a really long steep road and on to the pier, and I saw it, I could see the "End of the trail" sign. I walked up to it and stopped and looked at it, then I slowly put my right arm out and touched it, I had done it, I had finished Route 66 and I had done it on my own, and I did it my way!

I stood there with tears in my eyes I had done it I had driven a total of 2938 miles from Chicago to Santa Monica via Las Vegas in 10 days. I was tired and my mental state was all over the place, but I had done it. I walked down to the end of the pier and it was like being in the game GTA V. I could see where Baywatch was filmed, where Rocky 3 was filmed and wondered how many people had felt this feeling of accomplishment. Now you need to watch your arse here as the scams are rife! There are people walking around with beaded bracelets and they hand you one then refuse to take it back and demand a high price. The pickpockets are also out in force so whatever you do just be careful if you ever go here. I went to the official Route 66 hut at the end point and got myself a certificate, now you can't just get one of these not only do they quiz your knowledge but you need to prove you have done it. After this I was given my certificate and I've never felt happier, I called home and just started crying, I was dehydrated, extremely hot and overwhelmed.

I saw a bar and made a point of going in, I ordered a double Bushmills single malt Irish Whisky and a bottle of Cools light. This cost me $35.00 and I just stood there and laughed loud and slammed a $50 down and said "keep the change" like in the films. Now I'm not sure if it was the shock of the price but that was a big tip for me!

In America they serve the drinks different than in the UK I was first given the Cools light and the bottle had frost all over it then came the single malt Irish whisky. The whisky I was expecting like in the UK a little amount in a glass but not here, I was given a glass around the size of my crystal whisky glasses I have at home and it was filled to the top. I thought well this is a huge glass but here in the USA it's a normal double.

I got myself a seat looking out towards the pier and had a perfect cool breeze coming in from the sea keeping me cool. I sat there again people watching and feeling so proud of myself that I had done this trip on my own. I had not drank anything since breakfast 5 hours before so I made a start on the beer, I can tell you this beer was the best id ever had in my life! I drank it faster than I normally would back home but I had just finished my adventure and when in Rome and all that. I wanted to see some of the movie house locations around LA such as the Freddy house in the film a

nightmare on elm street, Halloween movie locations and where they had filmed The Fast and the furious films.
I drank the whisky and got my stuff and went to leave and BOOM I was on my arse laying on the floor, the glass smashed and the only other English in the bar that were at the back shouted out "yeahhhhhhhhhhhhhhhh" like we do back home in the UK.
I tried to get up and fell into a table and before I knew it two big American bouncers were lifting me up and dragging me outside. I was drunk beyond belief, drinking a bottle of beer followed by a big glass of strong single malt on a dehydrated semi empty stomach was a real bad idea, I thought that with my big frame id be ok but I was wrong, I was completely fucked!
I stood up and asked for my bag and camera and after what felt like an hour they gave it to me and I decided to head back to the car. Now heading up the steep road to the top of the Santa Monica pier was becoming a problem and I fell over again laughing at myself, then as if a gift from god himself, a few guys from a group of people who were preaching Bible quotes came over and helped me to the top the whole time I was laughing a bit like Phil Mitchell in the show Eastenders. They got me to the top told me I need Jesus in my life and went back, I was able to cross the road and headed up Colorado Ave and stumbled into a McDonalds where I was able to buy two double cheese burgers and a large coke. Now I can't fully remember what happened between me being given my food and the door

but the manager asked me to leave and guided me to the door. I walked back to the car and got in the back and left the door open so I would not cook myself. After eating the burgers and drinking the Coke I fell asleep and was woken an hour or so later by security informing me I was way over my time limit and I was asked to leave. I looked at the time and it was just after 4pm, I felt so pissed off with myself that I had wasted most of the day, but after the sleep I was feeling absolutely fine, not even a bad head. I made a start going around the Hollywood homes and my first stop was a nightmare on Elm Street. I could not believe I was actually here, I was standing at the house that I had been watching in films and TV shows since I was 10 and 30 years on I was standing right there.

After I went to see the houses used in the Halloween movie films and even got to see the famous hedge Michael Myers was standing behind.

This was pure heaven to me as I'm a huge horror film fan and I was so happy I could see them. I was able to see Dom's house from the Fast and the Furious films and maybe 100 meters down the hill you can see the location from Dom's shop from the first of the films. The day I was there one of the many cars used in the first film happened to be outside the shop and I was able to take some photos of it. Now this is not for everyone but I've always been a fan of famous graves so before it got too dark to do anything I headed to Pierce Brothers Westwood Village

Memorial Park & Mortuary where they have the most celebrity graves than any of the others.

I had seen videos of this place on YouTube and there were a few I really wanted to see. Some of the main ones I wanted to see were Dean Martin, Marilyn Monroe, Peter Falk, and Heather O'Rourke.

I actually saw the grave of Simpson's legend Sam Simon who boasted a Bart Simpson on his grave.

I walked around looking at all the graves of those who once made the world smile, laugh, cry and now they were here and once every now and then someone like me would pop by to say hello.

I did happen to walk by and notice the grave of Dominique Dunne who played the older sister of Heather O'Rourke in the film Poltergeist. Her grave was directly to the right of Heathers maybe 30 meters or so. I had read about the "curse" of the Poltergeist films but seeing both of their graves so close together was just so sad to see, they both died so young.

I won't carry on name dropping here but if you have an interest in it have a Google and check out my channel. After paying my respects for around two hours I made my way over to Beverley Hills where I was going to spend the night. I was expecting what I had seen in the films this tip top flash home to the rich and famous but what I got was in fact an American Oxford street filled with homeless living in tents on every street, and what looked like rough gang members. This was nothing like I had seen in fact I asked a cop if I was in Beverley Hills to which he replied "not what you expected right?" I just laughed and said "well yeah". I found the hotel and my room was more like a studio flat, I had a kitchen, huge fridge, living room area, bed area and a large shower and toilet. I left my stuff on the bed and went out to look for food. I walked across the road to a gas station and brought a turkey sandwich and some junk food and of course Pepsi. I wish they would sell the sandwiches here like they do in the USA; I had the choice of a turkey sandwich with either a mustard pack, with salt and pepper inside or mayo. It's such a strange feeling to take you're sandwich out and see little packets of salt and pepper and a sauce. I went back to my room had my little feast and made the choice to book a flight home for the next day. It was so expensive here and I was down to my last $800 and with the cost of petrol in LA, hotels, food even the parking it was not going to last me another week. I booked my flight with British airways and used the money I had left to pay towards it. I went to bed feeling good; the plan was to see the Hollywood sign and then head home. I woke up at 6am and checked my emails and saw that British Airways had gone on strike and my flight was cancelled. I was given the option to pay for my hotels and one meal a day and they would reimburse me at a later date but I never had the money to do this, I called home in a total panic I was fucked what was I going to do? British Airways were not taking calls and even if they could what was I going to do? The flights had all been cancelled. I had a quick shower and checked out as fast as I could. I jumped in Chevy Chev and headed to the Hollywood sign before driving to LAX airport. After an hour I found a place good enough to have a good look at the sign that was close enough to take a good photo. From here I headed to the airport driving through the Hollywood hills. It was some of the steepest and tightest turns I've ever driven on and it took me over 2 hours to get to LAX.

I saw the sign for Hertz rent a car and I dropped Chevy Chev off. I had driven a total of 3033 miles in total! I got my stuff out and at this point I was still mega pissed off and in a panic on how I was going to get home and what I was going to do, that I never said bye to the car. I know it sounds stupid and a bit mental but I had grown close to this car and had a bond the last four numbers on the licence plate were 8619, This also happened to be the last 4 numbers of my childhood home phone number that we had for 30 odd years. I think of this as fate! I was supposed to have this car, the total cost of petrol put in the car from Chicago to LA was $330.00 not bad ay? I wish I said thank you to Chevy Chev she was such a strong car that got me to the end with no issues apart from a missing aerial and a habit of only picking up the gospel radio stations 60% of the trip.

I got on a free bus that took me to terminal 3 and it was total chaos here, I was not the only one who wanted to get back to the UK and the shouting was real heated towards the staff.

I was told I would not be able to get back anytime soon so I looked at getting flights to France then I could get the Euro star to London but no luck. There were signs all over the airport to check the weight of your bags as there were heavy fines. I thought id check as the max weight I could have was 50kg and mine happened to be 65kg. I had been collecting toiletries from all the hotels and motels I had stayed in and I had to dump the lot in a bin. Boom still too heavy, I put my boots on and put my light trainers in the case and I dumped all my washing stuff even my tooth brush. The only thing I had left to make it bang on 50kg to lose was 3 bottles of Route 66 soft drinks and the bottle of champagne that British Airways had given me for my birthday and it turned out to be a blessing. I took the bottle of champagne and walked around and used my South London charm to buy some help. I saw a cleaner walking around and I made a point of going to him, I gave him the bottle of champagne and got talking to him, and he was the guy I needed. He told me Delta Airlines were putting on a flight that night and I should try them. He pointed me to the desk and I went over and just stood there till they opened.

After what felt life a lifetime a young lady came and opened up. I told her my problem and she checked and said "yes I have a seat available on the 10pm flight to London Heathrow" I said I'd take it then she said "that will be $2560" not realising at the time but British Airways were far from giving me a refund and I did not have enough money in cash or on my card to cover the cost. I then remembered I had a back up credit card that I'd never used it had a big enough limit to cover the costs. I got the card out and barely remembered the pin number but it went through and she took my case and handed me my boarding pass. I had a 12 hour wait at this point but I was going home!

I walked around and around drinking my Route 66 sodas that never tasted good at all really and I had kept the Root beer one to take with me through customs to drink on the other side. I was told there was a chance that I could go through to duty free early as I was on my own so thought I'd give it a shot. As I got close to the security the Root beer bottle fell out of my bag pocket and smashed. I just shouted "sorry" as I carried on walking to the security desk. They really seemed to check me on the way out and gave me a long search and went through my bag, at this point I started to sweat like I was actually doing something wrong. I was soon cleared and went through to the duty free area. I went to look for food and had the option of pizza or Chinese. I did want the Chinese but took the pizza option in case it gave me the shits. I had the pizza in a very crowded seating area and it was actually good. I went and sat around in different seating areas charging my phone and using the WIFI when it was not cutting out and asking me to pay every 15 minutes.

It got to around 6pm and I found myself in a bar by my gate, and I had a fruity IPA beer which was really nice. An American sat beside me who was going to Japan and asked me if it was a good beer and ordered one with a basket of fries. We had a laugh and talked about my trip and the trip he was just about to go on. We laughed about the size of his fries when they came out, and he seemed to really kick off that he had been ripped off, and all I could do was laugh. I never got his name but where ever he is I hope he had a great time. After drinking my bodyweight in IPA beers I again was very drunk. I made my way to the gate and sat there trying to sober up as I was scared they would not let me on. They moved us gates 3 times and it was a nightmare moving from one to the other then being told to head back all the while I'm trying not to fall over. I got to the final gate and saw I would be flying back on a Virgin Airways plane and I had always wanted to try Virgin so it was a win for me or so I thought. As I sat waiting I got talking to a couple who lived a few miles from my house and we got talking and having a laugh. I'd love to see these guys again if I could only remember their names; we sat and looked at the people who had not checked in at the second gate as the flight was way over booked and those without a seat number would not be flying to the UK.

I kept checking my ticket and my seat number over and over to make sure I was going home! The plane was pulled over to the gate and I looked to see what one it was and after waiting for them to get a bit closer I saw that our flight home was going to be on the Rosie Lee. They called the flight and I was up and ready. They seated all those in the more expensive seats and my drunken flirting to try get another free upgrade was no good at all as they had over sold by 70 seats.

I walked past the posh end then the semi posh end and before I knew it I was at my seat and I've never felt so big, I could hardly get my seatbelt on and there was no way I was putting my table down so I just looked out the window happy to be going home and worried about a 10 hour flight in one of the most claustrophobic situations I've been in since I was 13 and could not get my Rolla blades off. A young Spanish lady sat beside me and I just had to say sorry that she would not have enough room and as she said "its fine don't worry" a bigger lady came over and sat on the other side. I felt so bad for her. We took off on time and had a wonderful view of LA as the plane fly over and turned. It was soon time for the drinks and I asked for a coke and forgetting I was not in first I was given one of the mini cans and that was it for the whole flight, any other drink I would need to take a mortgage out on. I turned down the meal and put a red Virgin blanket over my head to try get some sleep and protect the crushed Spanish lady from my snoring. I only got a few hours and put the film Interstellar on which helped pass the time, and before I knew it they were doing a sort of breakfast, I opted for a

Blueberry muffin and the world's smallest plastic cup of warm pure orange, that may as well been a fucking thimble. The turbulence was the worst I've ever been in and at one point I did wonder if we were going to make it, I just sat there holding the muffin till I wanted it as I had nowhere to put it.

The muffin got everywhere I've never seen anything like it I dropped half of it on the floor and I was just past any stage of giving a shit.

We were flying lower and the sun was coming up and I could see land, I was almost home!

They announced they would be landing at 4pm and we all got ready, well everyone else but me who never took his belt off as Id not get it back on!

We landed!

I was home!

Or so I thought!

Due to strikes at Heathrow we now had a 3 hour wait on the tarmac as they had no baggage handlers to unload the planes, it was father's day and I just wanted to see my family. When we were able to get off the plane from hell we had another 6 hour wait for our luggage. At this point I was shouting at staff and I just lost it, it's the most angry I had been in years and I'm surprised I never spent the night in a cell. I was able to get us all cans of water as I started the whole human rights crap. Looking back I was a total prick, but I had just been left stranded in America and if I never had my emergency credit card I would have been fucked! Literary fucked with no place to stay, no money for food or drinks just stuck like Tom Hanks in the film The Terminal.

By the time I got my bag and made it to the coach station it was 1am. I was able to get a Mega Bus ticket cheap and slept the whole way home. This was a route I used to drive every day for work, so when I opened my eyes and saw I was 5 miles away I was over the moon!

I got a taxi from Bournemouth station home and I got to the door at bang on 3.15am. I was met by Jess and my Mum who had waited up for me. I woke the kids up as I had missed them so much!

2 days after I got home Natwest Bank sent me a HUGE box of 24 craft ales as a sorry for the security mix up, now that's what I call the best service! I think Carlsberg do banks after all?

This was a trip of a lifetime!

My adventure!

I had travelled America on my own in a 1ltr Chevy Spark and met some great people, and seen some of the most beautiful locations along the mother road. I had witnessed the most majestic views and done everything I always dreamed of doing.

I flew to America a mess of a man, and I found myself. I found who I was, and I found that out in the middle of the desert on Route 66.

I'm a sigma male with a heart to help others that can't help themselves.

There will be a few changes in my life; however I plan on living my life to the fullest and putting my family before anything and anyone.

I had to fly thousands of miles to find myself, to really put myself to the test to see what I'm made of and I am so much stronger than I knew I was.

Travelling alone is the most liberating thing I feel anyone can do. It's not to the weak or faint of heart but if you can just take that step, take that adventure you will feel so much stronger than you ever knew you could be.

Now if you decide to visit the USA there's a few things you need to know and keep in mind!

There's the rich and the poor, there are no middle ground people here.

Homelessness is a major issue in America, and I saw more closed and damaged shop fronts on Route 66 than I ever have in my life!

Keep in mind America is the murder capital of the Universe and have more serial killers than anywhere else, of course this doesn't mean you will be a target but I do feel there were a few situations that if I never had my size, beard and tattoos I could have been in some trouble.

I had this idea of the USA from TV and films but in reality it's NOTHING like it. Fruit is hard to find in most of the places I went to and when I did find apples they were really expensive. Chicago is one of the most dangerous places

I've ever been too so if you do decide to do Route 66 get to the stat sign and get west ASAP.

IT'S EXPENSIVE! Bottles of water were so over priced and most single person meals and were talking just a main meal no starters or sides will set you back around $20 unless you get fast food then it's just over half that.

You need to go to Hooters! Not just for the sake of going in one but the food is outstanding and it's a cheap place to eat, you really do get so much for your money!

Tipping is a thing here, they expect it across all of America, I was talking to one girl at a place I was eating and she said she needed the tips to live as she was on $2.00 an hour. I happened to of seen a Sonic up the road that was offering $12.00 an hour and wanted full and part time staff so I mentioned it and I was told "I shouldn't have to work there, I have a job here" so to me it looks like you just have to tip everyone.

TAX AND STATE TAX!!!!!

This was a real pain in my arse the whole time, the price you see on the ticket if NOT what you pay. When you get to the till they add tax and a state tax, this is different in EVERY state so I thought I was getting a deal on some sweets to take home but in fact it was more expensive, unlike the UK the price you see is what you pay, they like to make things really hard, so keep an eye out for that!

This book was my trip my way and in my words for the things I did, saw and experienced and should not be used as a guide.

This is the scariest thing I've ever done, but it's been one of the most fun adventures I've done!

I'll be doing Route 66 again for my 50th and my family will be with me on this one, and I'm looking forward to it. I was able to meet some of the nicest people I've ever come across and they would of done anything to help me, there are definitely more good people in America than bad, and its them that made my trip what it was.

The Adventure of a lifetime!

Hotels and Motels I used.

Sofitel London Heathrow
Terminal 5 London Heathrow airport, London TW6 2GD

Waldorf Astoria Chicago
11 E Walton St, Chicago, IL 60611, United States

Country Inn & Suites by Radisson,
Springfield, IL3092 Adlai Stevenson Dr, Springfield, IL 62703, United States

Super 8 by Wyndham
28 State Hwy P, Cuba, MO 65453, United States

Country Inn & Suites by Radisson
1034 North Garnett Road, Tulsa 74116 United States

Holiday Inn Express Hotel & Suites
101 East 13th Street, Shamrock Texas 79079 United States

Blue Swallow Motel
815 E, Route 66 Blvd Tucumcari New Mexico 88401, United States

Hotel El Rancho
1000 E hwy 66, Gallup New Mexico 87301 United States

The Lodge on Route 66
200 East Route 66 Williams Arizona
86046 United States

Las Vegas Hilton at Resorts World
999 Resorts World Ave, Las Vegas Nevada
89109 United States

Fairfield Inn & Suites
1041 East Harriman place
San Bernardino
92408 United States

Residence Inn by Marriott Beverley Hills
1177 South Beverley Hills drive
LA 90035 United States

Printed in Dunstable, United Kingdom